Spotlight SCIENCE 9

Keith JOHNSON   Sue ADAMSON   Gareth WILLIAMS

With the active support of: Lawrie Ryan, Bob Wakefield, Roger Walton, Gill Cox, John Dean, David Smith, Geoff Hardwick, Phil Bunyan, Jerry Wellington, Roger Frost, Kevin Sheldrick, Adrian Wheaton, John Bailey, Ann Johnson, Graham Adamson, Diana Williams.

Stanley Thornes (Publishers) Ltd

First published in 1995 by:
Stanley Thornes (Publishers) Ltd
Ellenborough House
Wellington Street
CHELTENHAM GL50 1YW
England

97 98 99 00 / 10 9 8 7 6

A catalogue record for this book is
available from the British Library.

ISBN 0 7487 1564 9

Typeset by Tech-Set, Gateshead,
Tyne & Wear.
Colour separations by Create Publishing
Services Limited, Bath.
Printed and bound in Spain by Mateu Cromo.

Acknowledgements

The authors and publishers are grateful to the following for permission to reproduce photographs:

Ace Photo Agency: Third Coast 36T, Mauritius 75B, 79C, Take Stock 109C, Roger Howard 142T;
Adams Picture Library: 64T, J Howard 116T;
Heather Angel: 13TL, TR;
Allsport: 122BR, Chris Cole 45BL, Bob Martin 45BR, 53B, Gary M Prior 45TR, Tony Duffy 48, Dan Smith 49, Shaun Botterill 50, Dave Rogers 51, Tom Hevezi 58, Michael Fauquet 56TR, Yann Guichaoua 72B;
Ardea London: J L Mason 138BL;
Associated Sports Photography: 72CC, George Herringshaw 72TL;
Barnabys Picture Library: 4CBR, 11, 14B, 18T, A Muttitt 13B, L Simpson 10B;
Biophoto Associates: 81B;
The BOC Group: 113C;
Britstock-IFA Ltd: West Stock Wanke 54;
BT pictures: 100R;
Bubbles Photolibrary: Ian West 22BR, Loisjoy Thurston 124T;
J Allen Cash Photolibrary: 13CL, 40TL, 76, 77, 87, 109TR, 132cR
Martyn Chillmaid: 4CTR, 22T, 25BR, 26, 28T, BR, BL, 32TL, B, 33, 34(5), 36BCL, BCR, BR, C, 37B, 37T, 40T, 42, 44T, 46T, B, 53T, C, 55T, 61, 64B, 66, 68, 69BR, 79T, 81T, 90, 91, 106, 108a, b, c, 109CR, BL, 110R, L, 111T, C, 112L, 113BL, 114(6), 116C, B, 117T, B, 119TR, TL, B, 117T, B, 118B, 119TR, TL, B, 122BL, 123, 128, 132b, cL, d, e, f, g, h, i, j, B, 133, 134R, C, L, 135(5), 136T, B, 138TR, TL, 139(5), 140c, d, e, f, g, 141T, B, 142B, 143TR, TC, TL, 145, 146, 150, 151, 154;
Bruce Coleman Limited: 137, Nicholas de Vore 36BL, Jane Burton 38T(g), 44CR, Peter Davey 18B, Frank Greenaway 69TC, Hans Reinhard 128BL, J Fennell 8T, Dr Frieder Sauer 12, Nigel Blake 138BR;
Collections: 113BR, 119C;
Mary Evans Picture Library: 29 Devany 158;
Eye Ubiquitous: Adrian Carroll 24L, Sue Passmore 143B, TRIP/TRIP 103BL, NASA/TRIP 103BR;
Geoscience Features Picture Library: 4CTC, 27L, R, 28BC, 38Tm, Tl, Tr, Tb, CR, BL, BR, 44CL;
Sally & Richard Greenhill: 74T, 78C;
Greenpeace: 4CL;
Robert Harding Picture Library: 24BL, 88T, 111B, 141C, FPG International 86T, M H Black 129, Walter Rawlings 72TR, Roy Rainford 152;
Holt Studios International: N Cattlin 4BL, 9B;
The Hutchison Library: 54T;
Image Bank: S Marks 80T, J P Fankhauser 15, Cover;
Impact Photos: 45TL, 73CL, 78B, 79B, 132T;
Kanehara & Co. Ltd: 64: Ishihara's Tests for Colour Blindness cannot be conducted with this material.
Frank Lane Picture Agency: 69TL, Celtic Picture Agency 39BR, R. Wilmshurst 22BL, R. Bender 128BR;
Last Resort: 40BR, 72CL, 88BR;
Magnum Photos: Chris Steele Perkins 4CBC, David Hurn 4CBL, W Eugene Smith 9T;
Milepost 9½ : British Rail Archive 110C;
Natural History Museum: 28CC;
Ontario Science Centre: 148;
Oxford Scientific Films Ltd: 130T, K A Larsson 5T, P Gathercole 13CR, C Milkins 13BL, JAL Cooke 13BR, M Chillmaid 14T;
PepsiCo International: 105;
Photo Library International Ltd: 101BL, 126;
The Photographers Library: 107T, 108TR;
Pictor International: 88BL;
Planet Earth Pictures: Barry Gorman 96, N Downer 4BR, F C Millington 8B, J Lithgoe 10T;
Paul Popper Ltd: 109BR;
Michael Powell/Times Newspapers Limited: 4T;
Mike Read 6;
The Science Museum/Science & Society Picture Library 31;
Science Photo Library: 74BL, BR, 75T, 80BL, BR, 125B, A & HF, Michler 28TL, S Stammers 38Ti, R de Guigliemo 38Tc, V Fleming 39BL, P Jude 44B, NPA 38CL, Dr R Clark & M R Goff 56TL, C Priest 69BL, CNRI 124B, 47TL, TCL, Dr J Burgess 127, D C R Salisbury 47TCL, A Pasieka 47TR, R Folwell 109TL, O Burriel 62, G Williams 25BL, A Hart-Davis 113T, 83, G Tompkinson 144B, ESA 101T, J Sanford 102, NASA 103T, S Fraser 156, R Ressmeyer 100L, 131, ESC 101BC, NRSC 101BR;
Sporting Pictures (UK) Ltd: 93
Tony Stone Images: 47B, 69TR, 86B, 112R, 122T, 140BL, Oliver Strewe 17, Eric Hayman 32TR, Terry Vine 55B, Chris Warbey 59, Peter Correz 71, J F Causse 72CR, Dan Smith 73TL, Jo McBride 73BL, L A Peek 121;
Telegraph Colour Library; 25T, 27C, 40R, 72T, 78T, 107B, 73CR, TR, BR, 85;
Topham Picture Source: 22BC, 125T, 140T, 144T, 147; 115;
Transport Research Laboratory/DOT: 89;
Viewfinder: 24C;
Wellcome Institute Library London: 82;
Wildlife Matters: 5B

Contents

Against all odds

This little boy stood for hours in the cold in London:
He wanted to tell people what had happened to his local river.

What do you think could have happened to the river?

This is just one example of **pollution**.
What do you think we mean by pollution?
Write down some of your ideas.

Pollution is when we do things that harm our environment.

What's causing the pollution?

Look at these photographs:

▶ Copy the list below of the types of pollution shown in the photographs.
Match each one with the correct effects from the other list:

Type of pollution	Effects of pollution
• dumping radio-active waste	• damages body cells
• oil spills	• lung diseases
• dangerous tips	• kills trees and water life
• smog	• kills sea-birds
• detergents	• harmful chemicals leak out
• acid gases	• too many water plants grow

Signs of pollution

When fossil fuels burn, they make acid gases like **sulphur dioxide**.
These dissolve in water in the clouds to make acid rain.
Acid rain can kill plants and fish.

Black spot is a mould that grows on roses. The mould cannot live if there is sulphur dioxide in the air.

a What does it tell you if roses do not have black spot?

Lichens are plants that are sensitive to sulphur dioxide in the air.

b Look at the shrubby lichens in the picture.
What do you think the air is like?

Who says the rain's to blame?

Does acid rain really damage plants?

Plan an investigation to see how acid affects the growth of cress seeds.

- What will you change?
- How will you make it a fair test?
- What will you measure to see if the seeds have grown?
- Your investigation should last about a week. How often will you record your results?

Show your plan to your teacher before you try it out.

No real answer

In Sweden, they are fighting acid rain by spraying lime on lakes.

c What do you think the lime does to the acid?

Experts say that it is "like taking aspirin to cure cancer".

d What do you think the experts mean by this?

e What would be a better way to cure acid rain?

1 Copy and complete:
Pollution occurs when .... put harmful ....
or energy into the .... When fossil fuels are
burned, they give off gases like ....
These gases dissolve in water to give ....
.... The effects of acid rain can be reduced
by adding .... to lakes.

2 Each day millions of cars pour poisonous
exhaust fumes into the atmosphere.
Pollutants in the fumes include lead, carbon
monoxide and nitrogen oxides.
a) Try to find out what effects these
chemicals have on our bodies.
b) How can these chemicals be reduced in
exhaust fumes?

3 Why do you think that people in
Norway blame factories in Britain for
acid rain pollution?
How could our factories give out less
sulphur dioxide?

4 Why do oil slicks appear on the sea?
What effect does oil have on sea-birds and
other coastal life?
How are oil slicks treated to make them less
harmful?

Things to do

Exploring pyramids

Food chains can show how food (and energy) pass from one living thing to another.

Write out this food chain in the correct order:

owl, oak leaves, shrew, caterpillar

a Where do the oak leaves get their energy from**?**

How many?

Food chains cannot tell you **how many** living things are involved.
It takes lots of leaves to feed a caterpillar, and lots of caterpillars to feed one shrew.

▶ Look at the diagram:

 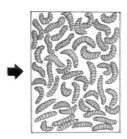 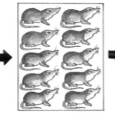

b Why are there more plants than there are herbivores**?**

c Why are there more prey than there are predators**?**

Up the pyramids

Look at the numbers in this food chain:

owl   1
shrews   10
caterpillars 100
oak leaves   300

You can show this information in a **pyramid of numbers**.
The area of each box tells us how big the numbers are.
Start with the plants on the first level and build it up:

level 4

level 3

level 2

level 1

▶ Copy the diagram and label each feeding level.

d What happens to the **numbers** of living things as you go up this pyramid**?**

e What happens to the **size** of each living thing as you go up this pyramid**?**

f Why are the plants always on the first level**?**

▶ Now try drawing a pyramid of numbers for each of these food chains:

	producer	herbivore	carnivore	top carnivore
g	5 cabbages	20 slugs	5 thrushes	1 cat
h	1 oak tree	100 caterpillars	5 robins	100 fleas

A top carnivore

Funnel fun

You can find very small animals in leaf litter using a **Tullgren funnel**.

- Set up the funnel as shown:
- Place a sample of leaf litter onto the gauze.
- Switch on the light and leave it for 30 minutes to work.
- *Be careful not to over-heat your sample and kill your animals.*
- Use a lens to look at the tiny animals that you have collected.

i What two things made the animals move downwards?

j Why should the light not be too close to your leaf litter?

k Why should your layer of leaf litter not be too thick?

Your teacher can give you a Help Sheet to identify your animals. It also tells you what they eat.

- Make a count of each of your animals and record it in a table:

Animal	Number found	Herbivore or carnivore?
mites springtails symphylids		

- Draw a pyramid of numbers for the animals you have collected.

Phew!... too hot and dry up there for me.

---

1 Copy and complete:
Pyramids of . . . . can tell us about the numbers of living things at each feeding . . . . Plants are always put in the . . . . level because they make food by . . . . and so bring energy into the food chain. As you go up the pyramid, the numbers of animals get . . . . and the size of each animal gets . . . .

2 a) Draw a pyramid of numbers from these data:

    sparrowhawk   1
    blue tits   5
    bark beetles 50
    beech tree   1

b) How is it that one tree can support so many herbivores?

c) Why do you think this is called an 'inverted pyramid'?

3 Instead of using numbers to draw pyramids, scientists sometimes use **biomass**. This is the weight of living material.
a) What would the pyramid of numbers in question 2 look like as a pyramid of biomass?
b) Draw and label it.

4 Look at the Help Sheet that you used in the activity on this page.
Choose 5 of the animals and make a key that you could use to identify each one. Get a friend to try it out.

Things to do

Dicing with death

Pesticides are chemicals that farmers use to kill **pests**.

a What kinds of plants and animals might be pests to a farmer?

b Why do you think farmers need to kill pests?

The main farm pests are insects, weeds and moulds.
Farmers need to control them because they destroy crops.

Nasty stuff

DDT is a pesticide. Only a small amount is needed to kill **any** insect.
It was used to kill plant pests and the mosquitoes that spread **malaria**.
However, DDT does not break down quickly. It stays in the soil for
a long time. So it can be passed along food chains. This is dangerous.

This lake in California was sprayed with DDT to control midges.
Look at the diagram to see what happened:

c How does DDT get into this food chain?

d What happens to the concentration of DDT as it passes along
the food chain? Try to explain this.

e Why are the fish-eating birds the first to be killed by DDT?

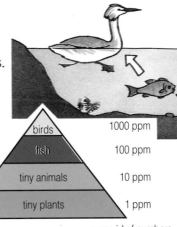

birds	1000 ppm
fish	100 ppm
tiny animals	10 ppm
tiny plants	1 ppm

pyramid of numbers

Who killed the sparrowhawk?

In the 1960s, seeds were often dipped in pesticide to protect them from pests.
Soon birds of prey, like the sparrowhawk, started dying.
Their bodies had large amounts of pesticide in them.
They also laid eggs with thin shells.

f How do you think the pesticide got from the seeds into the sparrowhawk?

g Why was it less concentrated in the bodies of seed-eating birds?

h Why do more birds die if their eggs have thin shells?

Pesticides, like DDT, are now banned in many countries.

The perfect pesticide?

A pesticide must be effective, but it must also be safe.
Discuss, in your groups, what makes a good pesticide.

- Which insects should it kill?
- For how long should it be active?
- Should it dissolve in water? Why?
- How will it get into the insect's body?
- On which part of the body will it act?
- How will it be safely used?

Write down your ideas.

Disaster in Minamata

Minamata is a fishing village in Japan. In 1953 there was a disaster. Fifty people died and hundreds were very ill. They were poisoned by mercury.

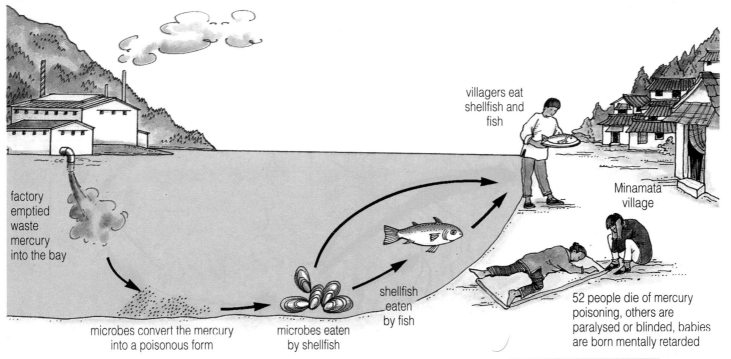

villagers eat shellfish and fish

Minamata village

factory emptied waste mercury into the bay

microbes convert the mercury into a poisonous form

microbes eaten by shellfish

shellfish eaten by fish

52 people die of mercury poisoning, others are paralysed or blinded, babies are born mentally retarded

▶ Look at the picture above.

i Where did the mercury come from?

j How do you think the mercury got into the food chain?

k Explain why the concentration of mercury was higher in the people than in the fish.

l What parts of the body are most affected by mercury poisoning?

1 Copy and complete:
Chemicals that kill pests are called . . . . Pests that can damage crops are . . . . , moulds and . . . . Some pesticides do not . . . . down easily. They can enter food . . . . and, as they are passed on, they become . . . . concentrated. Animals at the . . . . of the food chain are the first ones to die.

2 A new pesticide has been made to kill weeds.
The manufacturer wants to know at what concentration to sell it.
If it is too strong, it will kill the crop and harm wildlife.
If it is too weak, then it will not kill the weeds.
Plan an investigation to find out the best concentration of pesticide.

3 Some insects can develop **resistance** to a particular pesticide.
a) What is likely to happen to the farmer's crop if this happens?
b) What could the farmer do about it?

4 In Holland, they are using ladybirds to kill off lice on trees. The ladybirds are imported from California. Sixty million are being sold to Holland this year. The US suppliers say "Unlike pesticides, they are environmentally-friendly and real cute too!".
a) This is an example of **biological control**. What do you think this means?
b) What are the advantages of using ladybirds instead of pesticides?

Things to do

Cycles

Can you remember what happens to dead plants and animals?
They rot away. We say that they **decompose**.
The microbes that make dead things rot are called **decomposers**.
The most important microbes are **fungi** (moulds) and **bacteria**.

▶ Look at the diagram:

a How do plants take up nutrients?

b How do nutrients get into animals?

c How do nutrients get back into the soil?

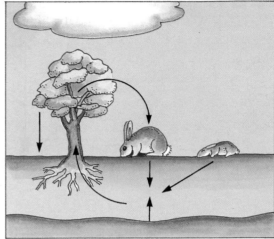

The natural roundabout

When plants and animals die, they decompose.
Nutrients are then put back into the soil.
Without fungi and bacteria, the dead material would never
decompose.

▶ Look at the diagram:

d Which process makes soil nutrients part of green plants?

e What are the living things that return nutrients to the soil?

We call the movement of nutrients a **nutrient cycle**.
This takes place on land, in fresh-water and in the sea.

f Where do you think the decomposers are found in the sea?

g Can you name 3 of the most important nutrients?

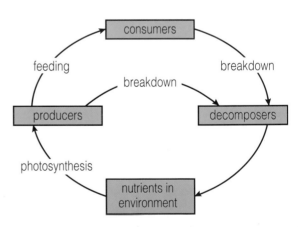

Natural or chemical?

Chemical fertilisers contain the nutrients **nitrogen**, **phosphorus**
and **potassium**. They are easy to store and to use. The farmer also
knows exactly how much of each nutrient is being used. However,
sometimes chemical fertilisers get washed out of the soil into rivers.
Some farmers prefer to use **natural fertilisers** like manure. They
rot down slower and add **humus** to the soil to improve it.

h Can you give 2 advantages of organic fertilisers?

i Can you give 2 advantages of chemical fertilisers?

How does a fungus feed?

Your teacher will give you 2 petri dishes containing starch-agar.
One has got a fungus growing in the centre of it.
The other has no fungus.

⚠️ eye protection

- Carefully lift the lids of each dish and pour in enough iodine to cover the agar. Replace the lids.
- Leave it for 1 minute, then pour away the excess iodine.
- Hold each petri dish up to the light in turn. What can you see?
- Make a drawing of each petri dish viewed against the light.

j What colour does starch go with iodine?

k Was there any starch around the fungus?

l What had the fungus made to break down the starch?

m How did these chemicals get to the starch?

- Carefully cut out some of the clear area.
  Test it for sugar by heating it with Benedict's solution.

n What colour do you think the Benedict's solution will go if sugar is present?

Keep on cycling!

Which of these things help to keep nutrient cycles going:

o Mowing the lawn and putting the clippings into a compost?

p Mowing the lawn and leaving the clippings on?

q Putting weeds into the dustbin?

r Spreading muck from a pigsty over a field?

---

1 Copy and complete:
Decomposers are microbes that . . . . down dead things. The most important decomposers are . . . . and bacteria. The nutrients in the soil are replaced when . . . . and animals die and . . . . Plants take up these nutrients and use them during . . . . Three important nutrients for plant growth are . . . . , phosphorus and . . . .

2 Have you ever seen a) a dead bird caught by a cat? b) a hedgehog run over on the road? c) a dead seagull washed up on the shore?
All these dead animals eventually disappear. Where do they go?

3 Which decomposes quicker: dead plant or dead animal material (a piece of meat)?
Plan an investigation to find out.

4 What would happen if there were no decomposers?
Write a story about what could happen if there were no fungi and no bacteria.

Things to do

Poison algae

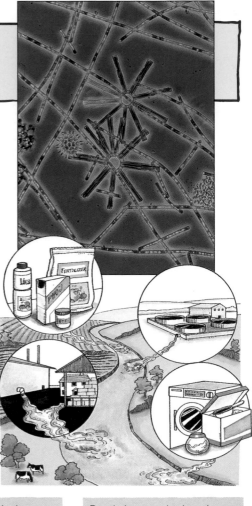

Algae are tiny plants. They live in lakes, rivers and seas.

Look at this food chain:

algae ➡ water fleas ➡ small fish ➡ large fish ➡ people

a Why are algae found at the start of the food chain?

b Can you name 3 things that algae need to grow?

c Why are fisheries often found where there are lots of algae?

Algae grow well when there is light, warmth and lots of **nutrients**.
Nutrients, like **nitrates** and **phosphates**, make algae grow best.

d What do you think will happen if *lots* of nutrients get into the water?

▶ Look at the picture:
Write down the ways in which *extra* nutrients get into the river.

Too much of a good thing

More nutrients mean more plant growth – in this case, lots of algae.
This can cause problems for animals and other plants in the water.

▶ Write out these sentences in the correct order.
They will tell you what can happen when too much algae grows.

Algae die and sink to the bottom of the lake or river.	Extra nutrients in the water make the algae grow fast.	The lack of oxygen in the water kills fish and other water animals.	Dead algae are broken down by microbes which use up lots of oxygen.

A soapy story

Detergents contain phosphates. These are plant nutrients.
In this experiment, you can find out the effect of detergent on the growth of algae.

- Label 6 test-tubes 1 to 6.
- Add 5 cm^3 of nutrient solution to each tube.
- Using a clean dropper, add 5 drops of algae water to each tube.
- Using clean droppers, add the following amounts of detergent solution and distilled water.

Test-tube	Drops of detergent solution	Drops of distilled water
1	0	5
2	1	4
3	2	3
4	3	2
5	4	1
6	5	0

- Leave all 6 test-tubes in a well-lit place.
- After a few days, shake each tube and see how green it is.
Compare the growth of algae in each one.
- Record your results in a table.
- Discuss your results and write down your conclusions.

Living indicators

We can use water animals to tell us how pure the water is:

- Come on in,
  the water's fine!

Mayfly larvae and stonefly larvae need clean water.

- It's getting worse!

Freshwater shrimps and water-lice can stand some pollution.

- The dirty duo!

Blood worms and sludge worms just love pollution!

e If you find a stonefly larva in a water sample, what would it tell you about the water?

f Which animals do you think could survive in the water in test-tube 6 in your investigation?

g Can you think of any other ways of testing the water for pollution?

---

1 Copy and complete:
Algae are . . . . that live in water. To grow well, they need light, warmth and . . . .
Two of the nutrients which increase the growth of algae are . . . . and phosphates. If too much algae grow, they die and . . . . rot them down. The microbes use up a lot of . . . . and this means that fish and other water animals will . . . .

2 Are farmers poisoning our water supply? Some of the nitrates in fertilisers wash out of the soil and trickle down into the bed-rock. Very slowly, the nitrates are moving nearer to water that we use to drink.
a) Try to explain the 'nitrate time bomb'.
b) Find out what effects nitrates can have on our health.

3 a) Should chemical fertilisers be banned?
b) What would happen to the world's food production if they were?
c) What could we use instead of them if they were banned?

Clearing weeds from a canal

Things to do

Questions

1 Every year, 250 tonnes of lead from fishermen's weights gets into the environment.
It is thought that birds like the mute swan eat the lead weights when feeding.
a) How do you think the lead gets into the blood of the swan?
Swans in town areas are more affected by this type of poisoning than those in the country.
b) Why do you think this is?
c) How could this pollution be reduced without banning fishing altogether?

2 The following data were collected from a river:
   pike   1
   trout   10
   water fleas   500
   algae   10 000
a) Draw a pyramid of numbers (not to scale) for the river.
b) Which living thing would you remove if you wanted to increase the number of trout in the river?
c) Give one other effect of removing this living thing from the river.

3 Some DDT was sprayed on a lake to control mosquitoes.
Look at the table showing the amounts of DDT in a food chain.

cormorant	26.5 ppm
pike	1.3 ppm
minnow	0.2 ppm
algae	0.05 ppm
water	0.000 05 ppm

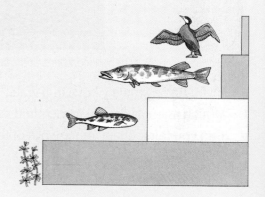

Explain how the cormorant has 500 000 times more DDT in its body than there is in the water.

4 The Royal Society for the Protection of Birds has said that more than 40 bird species are threatened by intensive farming. Birds in decline on farmland include the skylark, barn owl, lapwing and golden eagle.
a) List the ways in which you think farming can reduce bird numbers.
b) What steps do you think could be taken to improve this situation?

5 Plan an investigation to find out how clean your local river is.
What evidence of pollution would you look for?
What chemicals would you test for, and how?
How could you use 'indicator animals' to tell you how clean the river is?

6 Decomposers, like fungi, are very useful in the environment.
Explain why plants and animals depend upon them so much.

Energy

Without energy nothing can ever happen!

All living things need energy to stay alive and to move. You get your energy from your food.

Factories and transport need the energy that comes from fuels. And we need energy to heat our homes.

Go with energy

▶ Julie is playing with her group:

In the picture there are 8 forms of **energy** labelled.

a Write down the names of these 8 forms of energy.

Nuclear energy is not shown here. Add it to your list.

b What is nuclear energy?

Stored energy is called **potential** energy.

c Write down 3 examples of potential energy from the picture.

▶ What kind of energy has

d a stretched elastic band?
e a book on a shelf?
f a moving car?

Light energy (radiant energy) from the spotlights

When the drummer lifts her hands, she gives them **gravitational** potential energy

The lights and people are hot with **thermal** energy (heat)

Sound energy comes from the group

When the guitar string is stretched, it has **strain** potential energy

The people have movement energy (**kinetic** energy)

Electrical energy is needed for the lights and instruments

The people have **chemical** energy stored, from the food they have eaten

Energy diagrams

Here is an **Energy Transfer Diagram** for a torch:

g Copy and complete this diagram.

h Look at the numbers in the diagram. How many joules are transferred to light up the room?

i What is the *efficiency* of the torch?

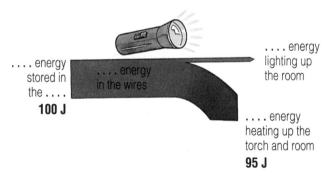

.... energy stored in the ....
100 J

.... energy in the wires

.... energy lighting up the room

.... energy heating up the torch and room
95 J

▶ A lot of energy is wasted in a car. For every 100 J of chemical energy in the petrol, only 25 J are transferred to kinetic energy. The rest just heats up the engine and the air.

j Draw an Energy Transfer Diagram for this, to scale.

This is what happens in energy transfers.
Although there is the same amount of energy afterwards, not all of it is useful.

This is summed up in the 2 laws of energy:

Law 1 The total amount of energy in the universe stays the same. It is 'conserved'. Energy cannot be created or destroyed.	**Law 2** In energy transfers, the energy spreads out, to more and more places. As it spreads, it becomes less useful to us.

Making electricity

One way to make electricity is to use the energy of falling water.
Your teacher can show you this:

The falling water turns a turbine, and this turns a dynamo.

This is like a **hydro-electric power station**, where the water is stored behind a dam.

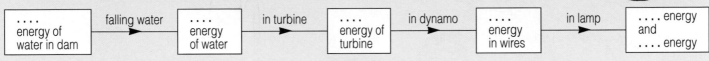

1 Falling water   **2** Turbine   **3** Dynamo   **4** Lamp in your house

k What form of energy does the water in the dam have? (Hint: it is high in the mountains.)

l Copy and complete the energy flow-chart for this:

.... energy of water in dam	→ falling water →	.... energy of water	→ in turbine →	.... energy of turbine	→ in dynamo →	.... energy in wires	→ in lamp →	.... energy and .... energy

m How could you make electricity from energy in the **wind**?

▶ Another way to make electricity is to burn a fuel, which boils water to make steam.
The steam then turns a turbine, and this turns a dynamo:

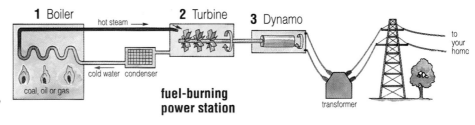

1 Boiler   hot steam →   **2** Turbine   **3** Dynamo   to your home

cold water   condenser

coal, oil or gas

fuel-burning power station

transformer

n Draw a flow-chart for this power station, like the one in question **l** above.

▶ Fuel-burning power stations cause pollution.
They give out sulphur dioxide and carbon dioxide gases.

o The sulphur dioxide dissolves in the rain to cause **acid rain**.
What effect does acid rain have on lakes, forests and buildings?

p Carbon dioxide 'traps' the Sun's energy and keeps the Earth warm.
This is called the **greenhouse effect**.
However too much carbon dioxide would be a bad thing for the Earth. Why? What do you think could happen?

Trees killed by acid rain

Things to do

1 Copy and complete:
a) Energy is measured in . . . .
b) The 9 forms of energy are:
c) Stored energy is called . . . . energy.
d) In any energy transfer, the total amount of . . . . before the transfer is always . . . . to the total amount of . . . . afterwards.
e) After the transfer, not all of the . . . . is useful.
f) Sulphur dioxide from power stations can cause . . . . rain, and carbon dioxide may warm up the Earth too much, because of the . . . . effect.

2 What are the energy transfers in
a) a Bunsen burner?   b) a television?
c) a yo-yo?   d) a hair-dryer?
e) a clockwork toy?   f) an apple tree?

3 In a nuclear power station, nuclear energy heats water to make steam. Draw a flow-chart for it, like the one shown above.

4 In one second a lamp transfers 100 J, but only 4 J is light energy.
a) Draw an Energy Transfer Diagram for it.
b) What is the efficiency of the lamp?

Energy from the Sun

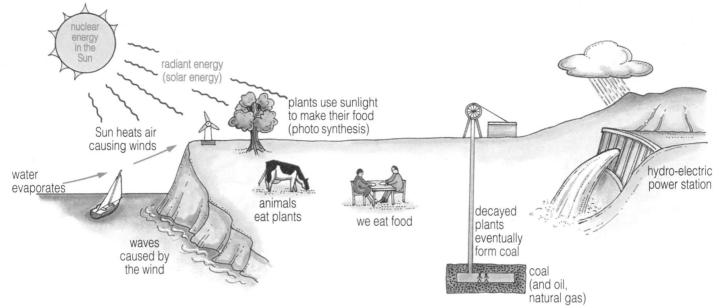

nuclear energy in the Sun

radiant energy (solar energy)

Sun heats air causing winds

water evaporates

waves caused by the wind

plants use sunlight to make their food (photo synthesis)

animals eat plants

we eat food

decayed plants eventually form coal

coal (and oil, natural gas)

hydro-electric power station

▶ We get most of our energy from the Sun.
Use the diagram to help you to answer these questions:

a In plants, what is the name of the process that transfers solar energy to chemical energy (food)**?**

b When you drink a glass of milk, it gives you energy. How did the energy get into the milk**?**

Here are some food-energy chains that are in the wrong order. Write each one in the correct order.

c humans, Sun, sheep, grass
d ladybird, rose, greenfly, Sun
e dead leaves, tree, Sun, blackbird, woodlouse

f Explain how water from the sea gets to the dam for this hydro-electric power station:

A hydro-electric power station

▶ Coal, oil and natural gas are called **fossil fuels**.
g Explain how i) coal, and
                    ii) oil and natural gas,
were formed. (Your teacher may give you a Help Sheet.)

h How can you heat a house using solar energy**?**
Draw a sketch to show how.

Plant and animal materials are called **biomass**.
Biomass can give us energy as food, and in other ways too.
For example, methane gas can be made from rotting rubbish or cow dung. Wood is used as the main fuel in many parts of the world:

Sources of energy

▶ Look at the pie-chart and answer these questions.

i What was the biggest source of energy in 1994?
j What was its percentage?

k Some fuels are **renewable**. What does this mean?
l Which 2 of these sources are renewable?

m There are 5 other renewable sources of energy.
Write down as many as you can.
n Why do you think these 5 sources are not shown?

o What is a **non-renewable** resource?
p Which of the sources in the pie-chart
are non-renewable?
q Which of them are fossil fuels?

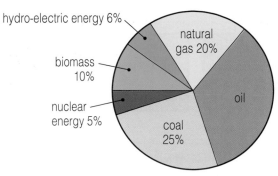

World energy sources in 1994

▶ The time-chart shows how long
the 3 fossil fuels are likely to last:

r How old will you be when the oil
runs out?
s Predict what you think the pie-chart
will look like when you are 60.

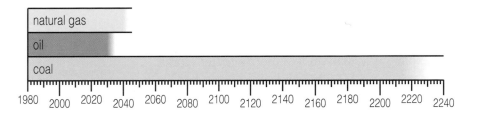

World trade in energy

The graph shows the energy sold commercially each year:

t Which of these sources is not shown in 1970?
u Why is biomass not shown at all?

v What happened to world demand during these 30 years?
w Estimate the world energy demand in 2010.

x Discuss what the graph will look like when you are 60.
Can you predict its shape?

y Draw a pie-chart for the year 2000.

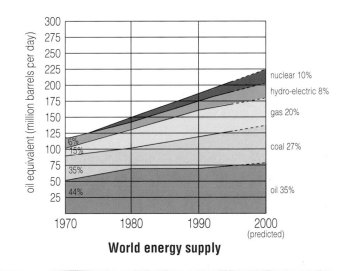

World energy supply

Reading the meters

Your teacher will give you a Help Sheet on which
you can record how much energy you use in your home.

1 Copy and complete:
a) Most of our energy comes from the . . . .
b) The Sun's . . . . is passed to plants and
. . . . by a food-energy chain.
c) Coal, ... and . . . . are fossil . . . .
d) Coal and . . . . and . . . . and uranium are
non- . . . . sources of energy.
e) The 7 renewable sources of energy are:

2 Do a flow-chart to show how energy in a
coal-mine makes a cup of tea for you.

3 Make a table showing how people could
save non-renewable fuels. For example:

Action to be taken	How it saves fuel
turn off the lights	uses less electricity

Things to do

Warming up with energy

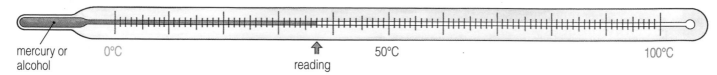

mercury or alcohol   0°C   ↑ reading   50°C   100°C

a What do you measure with a **thermometer?**

b What is the reading on this thermometer?
(This is the temperature of a human body.)

c What happens to water at i) 0°C?   ii) 100°C?

d Explain how you think a thermometer works.

Thermal energy

Thermal energy (heat) is **not** the same thing as temperature.
To understand this, let's compare these 2 things:

A white-hot spark

The tiny sparks are at a very high temperature, but
contain little energy because they are very small.

Each atom in the spark is **vibrating**.
Because it is very hot they are vibrating a lot.
But there are not many of them, so the total amount
of energy is small.

This idea about atoms is called the **Kinetic Theory**.

A bath-full of warm water

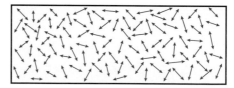

The water is at a lower temperature, but
it contains more energy.
This is because it contains more **atoms**.

Each atom is vibrating at a low temperature,
but there are many of them.
There is a lot of thermal energy (heat).

Warming up water

Plan an investigation to see what happens when you give
the same amount of energy to different amounts of water.

- How will you make sure that you give the **same**
  amount of energy each time?

- Show your plan to your teacher, and then do it.

- Explain what happens, using these words:
  energy   atoms   vibrating   temperature

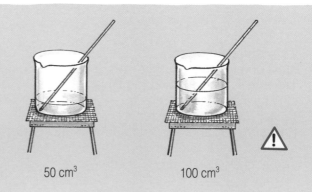

50 cm³   100 cm³

Energy on the move

Energy always travels from hot things to cold things.
There are 3 ways that the energy can travel:

Conduction

The metal handle gets too hot to hold.
The energy has been **conducted**
through the metal.

The metal is a good **conductor**.
The wooden spoon is an **insulator**.

Convection

The air over the heater is warm.
The hot air is rising upwards, in
convection currents.

You get similar convection currents
when you heat a beaker of water.

Radiation

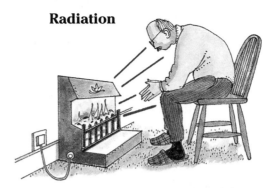

Radiant energy is travelling through the
air, just like solar energy from the Sun.

The rays can travel through space, at
the speed of light. They are also called
infra-red rays.

▶ Here is a picture of a Bunsen burner heating up some gauze:

e After a while, the base feels warm at the point A. Why is this?

f If you put your hand at point B, it is hot. Why is this?

g If you put your hand near the red-hot gauze, at point C, it
feels warm. Why is this?

▶ Here is a 'model' to help us see the difference between these 3 ways.
Three ways of getting a book to the back of the class:

1 Conduction: you can pass a book
from person to person – just as the
energy is passed from atom to
atom.

2 Convection: you can carry the book
to the back of the class – just as hot air
moves in convection, taking the
energy with it.

3 Radiation: a book can be thrown
to the back of the class – rather like
the way energy is radiated from a
hot object.

---

1 Copy and complete:
a) When an object is heated, the energy
makes the . . . . vibrate more. The hotter
the object, the more the . . . . vibrate.
b) Energy travels from hot objects to . . . .
objects by . . . . , or . . . . , or . . . .

2 Explain why a white-hot spark falling
into a bath of water does not make the
water hot.

3 Explain how an electric fire heats up a
room.

Things to do

Conduction

▶ What would you feel if you stirred some hot soup with a metal spoon and with a wooden spoon? Can you explain this?

Energy on the move

- Set up 3 rods as shown, of copper, iron and glass:
- Use vaseline to fix a drawing-pin at the end of each rod.
- Then heat the ends of the rods equally, with a Bunsen burner.
- What happens? How long does it take for the first and second pins to fall off?

copper
iron
glass

a Which way was energy flowing in the rods?

b Does the energy flow at the same rate through all the rods? Explain your answer.

c Which of these 3 materials would be best for making a pan? Explain your answer.

▶ The diagram shows how we can explain conduction, using the idea of atoms:

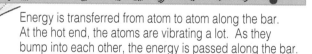

Energy is transferred from atom to atom along the bar. At the hot end, the atoms are vibrating a lot. As they bump into each other, the energy is passed along the bar.

▶ As you saw, copper is a good **conductor**. In fact, **all metals are good conductors**. Glass is an **insulator**. Air is a very good insulator. We use this to keep us warm:

Birds fluff up their feathers in winter, to trap more air. The air is a good insulator and keeps them warm.

An anorak has a lot of trapped air. This slows down the transfer of thermal energy from your body.

Insulation in the loft of your house keeps you warm, and saves money. The material contains a lot of air.

Keeping warm

Your teacher will give you some materials that could be used for clothes, or to insulate your house.

Your job is to find out which of these materials is the best insulator.

- What equipment will you use?
- How will you make it a fair test?
- How will you record your results?
- Show your plan to your teacher, and then do it.

- Which material is best?
  Why do you think it is best?

hot water

Saving energy at home

Here are 2 houses:

One of them has been carefully insulated.

d Which house has **not** been insulated?

e What is the total heating bill for this house?

f Imagine you lived in this house.
Which parts would you insulate first?

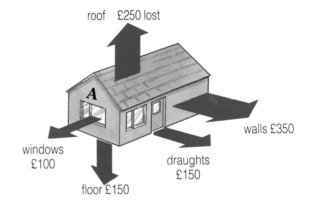

roof £250 lost

A

windows £100

walls £350

draughts £150

floor £150

g What is the total heating bill for the insulated house?

h All these places have been insulated:
walls, roof, floor, doors, windows.
- Put them in order of the money saved.
- Next to each one, write the amount of money saved.

i Draw an Energy Transfer Diagram for each house.

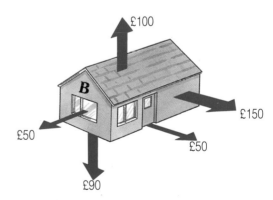

£100

B

£50

£150

£50

£90

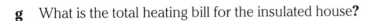

Things to do

1 Copy and complete:
a) All metals are good . . . .
Copper is a very good . . . .
b) Glass is an . . . .
Air is a very good . . . .
c) Thermal energy passes through the bottom of a pan by . . . .
The energy is passed from each vibrating atom to the next . . . .

2 Make lists of where a) conductors and b) insulators are used in your home.

3 Write a letter to a pupil in your last school explaining what conduction is.

4 A double-glazed window has 2 sheets of glass, with air between.
Plan an investigation to see if double-glazing helps to insulate.
(Hint: you could use a beaker inside a bigger beaker.)

5 Explain this statement: "All the energy used in heating our homes is wasted."

Convection and radiation

Convection

Have you ever noticed that flames always go upwards?
This is because hot air is lighter than colder air.
The hot air rises.

hot air rises

a Where is the hottest part of the room – the floor or the ceiling? Why?

b Why does smoke go up a chimney?

- Fill a beaker with cold water.
- Very gently, place a crystal of purple dye at the bottom and near the side:
- Put a **small** flame under the crystal.

- What happens? Explain what you see.

The water moves in a **convection current**.
This carries the energy round the beaker.

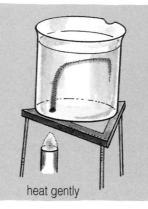
heat gently

▶ You get the same thing in a room.
The room is heated by the convection currents moving round:

c Why does a hot fire sometimes give you a cold draught on your feet?

On a sunny day, hot air currents can rise from the ground. Glider pilots can use them to lift their wings.

The Sun can cause very large convection currents, which we feel as **winds**.

▶ Use what you know about convection currents to explain what is happening in these photos:

convection current

Radiation

This sun-bather is getting hot:
Her body is **absorbing** energy.

d Where is the energy coming from?

e Could the energy have reached her by conduction or convection? Explain your answer.

This energy is called **solar energy** or **radiant energy**.
The rays include **infra-red rays** and **ultra-violet rays**.

f How can you use solar energy to cook food?

▶ Our bodies also **emit** (give out) radiation.
We **radiate** energy.
This is shown on the thermogram:

g Which part of the man is giving out
  i) the most energy?
  ii) the least energy?

h Use the key to estimate the temperature of his cheek.

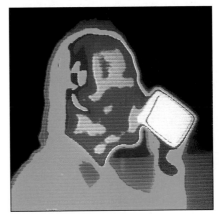

☐	above 38°C
	35°C
	32°C
	29°C
	26°C
	below 23°C

Melanie and Chris are discussing the colour of cars.

Melanie says, "I think black cars get hotter in the Sun."
Chris says, "Silver is brighter – I think a silver car will get hotter."

Plan an investigation to see who is right.

- How will you make it a fair test?
- How many readings will you take?
- How will you show your results?

Show your plan to your teacher before you do the investigation.

1 Copy and complete:
a) Thermal energy can be carried through a liquid by a . . . . current. The hot liquid . . . . and the . . . . liquid falls.
b) . . . . currents also flow in air.
c) . . . . rays travel from the Sun through empty space. This energy is called . . . . energy or . . . . energy.
d) A black object absorbs more . . . . than a silver one.
e) A silver surface . . . . the rays like a mirror. This is used in a . . . . cooker.

2 Explain why:
a) Food cooks faster at the top of an oven.
b) Fire-fighters enter smoke-filled rooms by crawling.
c) Houses in hot countries are often white.
d) There is shiny metal behind the bar of an electric fire.

3 A potato is being cooked in boiling water. Explain, as fully as you can, how energy gets from the gas flame or hot-plate into the middle of the potato.

Things to do

25

Questions

1 The diagram shows some of the energy transfers that take place in a hair-dryer during one second:

a) Not all the energy transfers are shown in the diagram. Explain how you can tell this.

b) Draw an Energy Transfer Diagram of this, and label it.

c) What happens eventually to all the energy?

2 When you switch on a light, it is the result of a long chain of events. These are listed, but in the wrong order. Write them down in the correct order.

A   plants change to coal over millions of years
B   the Sun produces energy
C   water is heated, to make steam
D   the plants die
E   plants take in solar energy
F   the energy is radiated, and travels to the Earth
G   coal is burnt in oxygen (in air)
H   steam makes a turbine turn
I   the generator produces electricity
J   electricity heats up the lamp and it shines
K   electricity travels through wires to your home
L   the turbine turns a generator

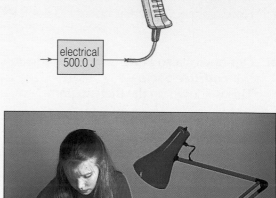

3 Jo has 2 mugs. They are the same except that one is black and one is white. They were filled with hot coffee and allowed to cool. Jo took their temperatures every 2 minutes, as shown in the table:

a) Plot a graph (of temperature against time) for each mug, on the same axes. Draw the lines of 'best fit'.

b) Which result do you think is wrong?

c) What is the temperature of the black mug after 3 minutes?

d) What is the difference in temperature after 9 minutes?

e) What conclusion can you draw from the graphs?

Time (min)	Black mug (°C)	White mug (°C)
0	90	90
2	68	78
4	55	67
6	45	58
8	37	52
10	31	43
12	26	37

4 The diagram shows a solar panel. It is using solar energy to heat water:

a) Which way is the water flowing in the pipe?

b) Why is the hot water outlet at the top of the tank?

c) Using the idea of atoms, explain how energy is transferred through the wall of the pipe to the water in the tank.

d) Why is there a black surface in front of the pipe and a shiny surface behind it?

e) Explain, step by step, how energy is transferred from the Sun to the hot water tap.

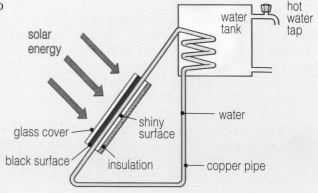

Elements, mixtures and compounds

Everything around you is an element, a mixture or a compound.
You are a combination of elements, mixtures and compounds.
The elements are the building blocks.
There are 92 natural ones. How many can you name?

In this topic you will be looking at lots of elements.
Some will be in mixtures . . . . Some will be in compounds . . . .

▶ Do you remember classifying in Book 7?
How are books classified in your school library?
How are compact discs classified in a music store?

Scientists have a way of classifying **elements**. It is called the **periodic table**.

a What is an element?

You've met lots of elements already.
Which of the elements in the box:

b rusts?

c has the symbol H?

d has the symbol S?

e has the symbol Cu?

f turns blue with starch?

g is about 21% of the air?

All these elements are in the periodic table.
But how are they arranged?
Let's look for patterns.

Elements
copper
iron
hydrogen
iodine
oxygen
sulphur

The elements here are sodium, gold, copper, chlorine and sulphur. Can you identify each one?

Grouping elements

Look at this information about elements.

Element	Melting point in °C	Boiling point in °C	Appearance	Reaction with cold water	Other information
sodium	98	890	silver-grey solid	reacts violently	conducts heat and electricity
silver	960	2212	shiny silver solid	no reaction	conducts heat and electricity
helium	−270	−269	colourless gas	no reaction	very unreactive, doesn't conduct
lithium	181	1330	silver-grey solid	reacts very quickly	conducts heat and electricity
copper	1083	2595	shiny pink-brown solid	no reaction	conducts heat and electricity
chlorine	−101	−34	green-yellow gas	dissolves	reactive, doesn't conduct
argon	−189	−186	colourless gas	no reaction	very unreactive, doesn't conduct
fluorine	−220	−188	pale yellow gas	dissolves	very reactive, doesn't conduct
gold	1063	2966	shiny gold solid	no reaction	conducts heat and electricity
potassium	63	765	silver-grey solid	reacts very violently	conducts heat and electricity
neon	−250	−246	colourless gas	no reaction	very unreactive, doesn't conduct
bromine	−7	58	red-brown liquid	dissolves	reactive, doesn't conduct

Make a data card for each element. Use your cards to match up similar elements. You can move the cards around to get the best match.

• Which elements have you grouped together? Why?

• Within each of your groups, put the elements in order.

• Explain your order.

DATA CARD

Element _____
Appearance _____

Melting point _____
Boiling point _____
Reactivity _____

Mendeleev was a Russian scientist. In 1869 he made a pattern of elements. He put elements in **groups**.
This pattern is called the **periodic table**.

Your teacher will show you a copy of the **periodic table**.
The columns of elements are called **groups**.
The rows of elements are called **periods**.
Are *your* groups the same as those in the periodic table?

h Which elements are in the same group as chlorine?

i Name 2 elements in the same period as chlorine.

On your copy of the periodic table you can see numbers. Each element has a number. This is called the **atomic number**. What does the number tell us?

Inside the atom

All materials are made up of **atoms**. Atoms contain both positive and negative charges.
The diagram shows what we think an atom is like:
At the centre of the atom are tiny particles called **protons**.
These are positive. The negative charges are in the outer parts of the atom.

j How many protons are there in the diagram?

The atomic number tells you the number of protons in the atom.
▶ Look at your periodic table.
All helium atoms have 2 protons.
All carbon atoms have 6 protons.

k How many protons are there in each oxygen atom?

l Which element has twelve protons?

Atoms of the same element have the same number of protons.

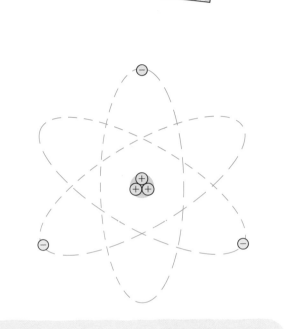

Video highlights

The Spotlight Video Company needs your help.
The company wants to make a new video.
It will be about elements and the periodic table.

- The video will be for 13-year-old pupils.
- It should be about 5 minutes long.
- It should be interesting and exciting. (It *might* be funny!)
- It should explain about elements and the periodic table.

Your group should write a script for the video.
What will be seen on the screen? Explain what filming will be needed.
Who would you like to present your video? Money is no object!

Things to do

1 Copy and complete:
a) Elements are classified in the . . . . table.
b) The columns of elements are called . . . .
c) The rows of elements are called . . . .
d) Atoms of the same element have the same number of . . . .

2 Name 2 elements in each case which are: a) solids b) liquids c) gases.

3 Choose one group of elements. Use books to find out about the group. Make a wall poster about the elements.

A burning tale

500 B.C.

The Greeks thought that the universe was made from 4 elements: fire, water, air and earth.
They believed **everything** was made of these elements.

So what happens when something burns?

The fire is released.

The water and air escape.

The earth or ashes are left behind.

EARTH
AIR · FIRE
WATER

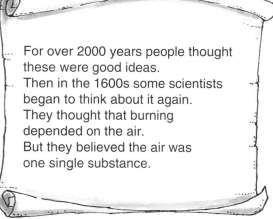

For over 2000 years people thought these were good ideas.
Then in the 1600s some scientists began to think about it again.
They thought that burning depended on the air.
But they believed the air was one single substance.

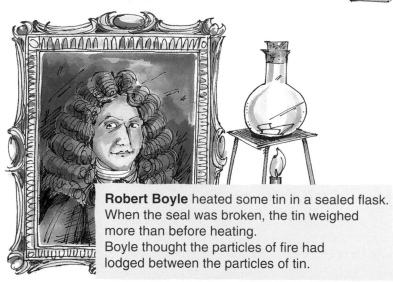

Robert Boyle heated some tin in a sealed flask.
When the seal was broken, the tin weighed more than before heating.
Boyle thought the particles of fire had lodged between the particles of tin.

Georg Stahl (1660–1734) was a German scientist. He developed another idea. It was called the phlogiston theory (from the Greek phlox=flame).

Every substance that burns has 2 parts — ash and PHLOGISTON.

When something burns the PHLOGISTON escapes. The ash is left behind.

But this burnt charcoal has only left a little ash.

That's because it contains so much PHLOGISTON!

In the early 1700s, the phlogiston theory was thought to be a great idea. But it didn't explain everything. Many materials like Boyle's tin, **gained** weight after heating. They should have been *losing* phlogiston. The theory must be wrong.

Antoine Lavoisier was a French scientist. He worked with his wife. Together they worked on the problem of burning. They knew the phlogiston theory wasn't quite right.

Something is wrong here!

Lavoisier heated sulphur. He found that the sulphur gained weight when it burnt. He thought the air was combining with the sulphur. But it needed a visit from **Joseph Priestley** in 1774 to help Lavoisier to understand.

This is the piece of apparatus Lavoisier used for his early burning experiments. How do you think it works?

Joseph Priestley worked in England. He heated mercury in air. He made a red substance. When he heated the red substance he got a new gas.

This gas lets things burn very brightly in it.

Priestley went to France to tell Lavoisier about the gas. Lavoisier repeated and improved Priestley's experiments. He soon understood the results. Air must be more than one gas. One gas is needed for burning. This is oxygen. When a substance burns, it combines with the oxygen in the air.

NOW I understand air can't be just one gas.

MERCUR

Things to do

1 Read about Robert Boyle's experiment.
a) Suppose Boyle had reweighed his heated flask **before** breaking the seal. What do you think he would have found?
b) Why did the flask weigh more **after** the seal was broken?

2 Supporters of the phlogiston theory argued strongly with those who disagreed. Write a cartoon strip to show an argument between 2 scientists in the 1700s. One scientist believes the phlogiston theory, the other does not.

3 Lavoisier was sentenced to death after the French Revolution. He had become a hated tax collector for the government. Revolutionaries wanted him dead. The judge said "The Republic has no need of men of science." Do you think your country has "no need of scientists?" Explain your views.

4 Lavoisier found that only some of the air was used up when mercury was heated in air.
a) Design some apparatus which he could have used to show this.
b) What percentage of the air is oxygen?
c) Oxygen is a very useful gas. How is pure oxygen separated from the air?

Two's company

Lego can make lots of different things.
The pieces are building blocks.

A few **elements** can make lots of **compounds**.
The elements are the building blocks.

In Book 8 you learnt about elements and compounds.

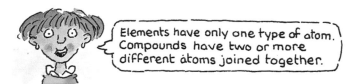

Elements have only one type of atom.
Compounds have two or more different atoms joined together.

Legoland

a Which boxes contain the elements?

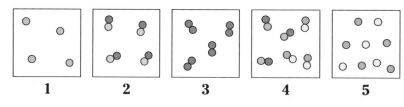

| 1 | 2 | 3 | 4 | 5 |

▶ Here are some formulas for compounds. See if you can work out their names.

b MgO
c $CuCl_2$

d HCl
e FeO

f CO_2
g H_2O

▶ Look around the room.

h Write down some of the compounds you can see.

i Write down some of the elements you can see.

Most elements are not found on their own. They are in compounds.

Some common compounds

Making a compound (1)

Take a piece of clean copper foil.
Hold it in tongs.
Heat it in a medium Bunsen flame for about 3 minutes.
Take it out of the flame.
Leave it to cool on a heat-resistant mat.

⚠ heat
eye protection

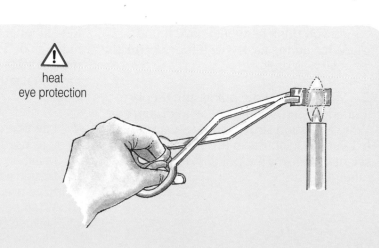

j Write down everything you see.

k Is there a reaction?

l Copy and complete this word equation:

copper + oxygen ⟶ ....
　　　　(from air)

Making a new compound (2)

Half fill a test-tube with dilute sulphuric acid.
Add one spatula measure of copper oxide.
Stir the liquid.
Leave the tube in your rack for 5 minutes.

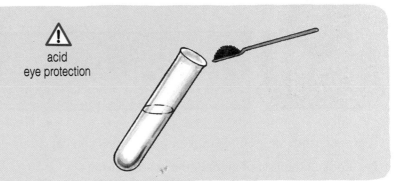

acid
eye protection

m Write down everything you see.

n Is there a reaction?

Making a new compound (3)

Half fill a test-tube with copper sulphate solution.
Put a piece of zinc into the tube.
Stir the liquid.
Leave the tube in your rack for 5 minutes.

eye protection

o Write down everything you see.

p Is there a reaction?

q Copy and complete this word equation:

   . . . . + copper sulphate ⟶ zinc sulphate + ...

Breaking compounds

When elements join together they make compounds.
It is not easy to get the elements back.

Look at this sample of copper sulphate crystals:

It contains copper, sulphur and oxygen. How could you get the
copper out? Discuss this in your group. Write down some of your
ideas. Your teacher may let you try some of them.

---

1 Copy and complete:
a) . . . . have only one type of atom.
b) . . . . have 2 or more different atoms
    joined together.
c) The formula of . . . . is MgO.
d) Copper can react with oxygen in the air.
    The word equation is:
    . . . . + ... ⟶ . . . .

2 Draw a table like this:

Element	Compound

Put these in the correct column:
chlorine   glass   gold
sugar   iron oxide   sulphur
carbon   copper sulphate

3 Look at Ann's science homework.

> I lit a spill. I put it into a tube
> of hydrogen gas. The gas
> reacted with oxygen in the air.
> I saw a flash. I heard a 'pop'
> sound. I made some water
> in the tube.

From Ann's work:
a) Write the names of 2 elements.
b) Write the name of 1 compound.
c) Was there a reaction?
    How do you know?
d) Write a word equation.

Things to do

It's a fix

Elements and compounds make up the foods you eat.

▶ Look at the lists of ingredients in some foods.
Can you match each list with the right food?
It's tricky. Some key ingredients have been missed out!

a
water
butter
cream
wheat flour
modified maize
   starch
dried skimmed
   milk
salt
spices

b
glucose syrup
sugar
pectin
citric acid
sodium citrate

c
tomato
water
onion
vegetable oil
malt vinegar
salt
garlic
paprika

d
maize
sugar
malt flavouring
salt
niacin
iron
folic acid
vitamin B$_6$
vitamin D

e
sugar
whey powder
calcium acetate
skimmed milk
lactose
fumaric acid
beta carotene
dried glucose syrup
salt

How much of each?

Compounds are made when elements join together.
But **how much** of each element?

Magnesium reacts with oxygen in the air.
But how much of each reacts?

Look at the diagram. This apparatus could help you find out.

magnesium + oxygen ⟶ magnesium oxide

In this experiment you need to know how much magnesium you start with. You then need to know how much magnesium oxide you make.
How do you think you can do this using the apparatus drawn?
Discuss this in your group.

Your teacher will give you an instruction sheet.
Read through all the instructions before you start.
This is a difficult experiment. Your results will tell your teacher how well you have done it!

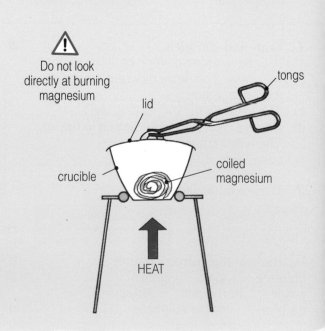

⚠️ Do not look directly at burning magnesium

HEAT

How much of each? – The results

Each group should have a result. Your teacher will collect these from all the groups.
Copy the class results into a table like this one:

Group	Mass of magnesium at start in grams	Mass of magnesium oxide at end in grams
A		
B		
C		
D		

Draw a graph of the results.

Mass of
magnesium
oxide

0

0   Mass of magnesium

What do you notice? Can you see a pattern in your results?

Magnesium reacts with oxygen. The masses of each element which combine are in **proportion**.
A fixed amount of magnesium always combines with a fixed amount of oxygen. The compound has **fixed composition**.
The compound always has the formula MgO.

▶ Copy and complete the table. The first one has been done for you.

Name	Formula	Number of each type of atom
aluminium chloride	$AlCl_3$	1 aluminium 3 chlorine
magnesium oxide	MgO	
sodium fluoride	NaF	
	CuO	
	H_2O	
		1 carbon 4 chlorine

Things to do

1 Copy and complete:
Compounds have . . . . composition. They have a fixed formula. The . . . . for carbon dioxide is CO_2. It has . . . . carbon atom and . . . . oxygen atoms.

2 Draw a room where you live. You can draw people and furniture in your room. Label 10 objects in the room.
Say what they are made from.
Say whether they are elements or compounds.

3 Luke made a graph of some class results.

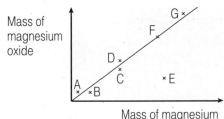

Mass of
magnesium
oxide

Mass of magnesium

a) Which group had a strange result? What do you think went wrong?
b) Which 2 groups started with the same amount of magnesium?

Mixed or fixed?

▶ Look at these ideas about mixtures and compounds.

Made of 2 or more substances

One substance only

Composition can vary

Easy to separate into elements

Fixed composition

Difficult to separate into elements. A reaction is needed.

Draw a table like this:
Write each idea in the correct column.

Mixture	Compound

Lots of natural substances are mixtures.
Some are mixtures of elements. Some are mixtures of compounds.
Often the mixtures must be separated before we can use them.

a How could you improve the water?

b Which gas is in Lisa's balloon?

c How could you get the petrol?

▶ Look at these photos. They are about mixtures. Can you explain the separations?

This is a hot country.
You can get salt from sea-water.

d How is the salt separated from the sea?

Salt is sodium chloride NaCl.

e Will it be easy to get chlorine from salt? Explain your answer.

This is a filter coffee maker.

f How does it work?

g How can you get the cream from the milk?

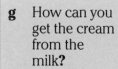

This is a machine to separate blood cells from plasma.

 h Which part is the plasma?

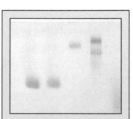

These are hospital tests on a child's urine.

i What is this process called?

A complete wreck

Read this extract from the *Dove Times*.

Experts were worried last night. A strange mixture was found on Dove Beach. A local man thinks it is from the ship *The Red Lady*. It was wrecked a few months ago down the coast. It was made of iron. It carried a cargo of salt and limestone. But sand from the beach may be in the mixture too.

Plan an investigation to get the pure substances from the mixture.
Try to get pure iron, salt and sand.
Show your plan to your teacher.
If it is safe, you can carry out your investigation.

Things to do

1 Copy and complete.
Choose a word from the box:

mixture	easy	element
hard	compound	

a) A mixture is . . . . to separate.
b) A . . . . has fixed composition.
c) A . . . . consists of 2 or more substances.
d) In a . . . . the elements or compounds do not combine.

2 Look at the properties of A, B and C.
How would you separate a mixture of them?

Substance	Dissolves in cold water?	Dissolves in hot water?
A	✗	✓
B	✗	✗
C	✓	✓

3 Why can we use this to strain tea but not coffee?

4

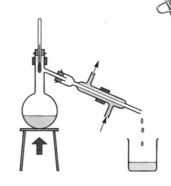

This apparatus gets pure water from sea-water.
a) Copy the diagram. Label the apparatus.
b) What is the process called?
c) Explain the process. Use the words: evaporate, condense.
d) What does the thermometer do?
e) How do you know the water is pure?

Mixtures and rocks

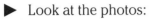

The photos show minerals and rocks.
Do you know the difference?

A **mineral** is a single substance. It has a formula.
It has a name.
But most **rocks** are **mixtures**. They contain
different minerals.

▶ Look at the photos:

a Which do you think are minerals?

b Which do you think are rocks?

Malachite

Limestone

Rock salt

Basalt

Iron pyrites

Calcite

Granite

Rock types

There are 3 main types of rock.
Read the sentences for each type of rock. They describe how the
rock forms. Put them in the right order. Copy out your answer.
The rock cycle opposite will help you.

Igneous
- Inside the Earth is **magma**. This is very hot molten rock.
- The volcano erupts. Magma comes to the surface of the Earth.
- Lava cools quickly. It makes igneous rock with small crystals.
- Some magma does not get to the surface. It cools slowly underground.
- Lava is the name for magma which comes to the surface.
- It turns to solid. It makes igneous rocks with large crystals.

Sedimentary
- Rocks at the surface can crumble. They make small particles.
- The lower layers get pressed together. They slowly form solid rock.
- The particles are carried away by rivers or wind.
- Other layers get put on top of them.
- The particles settle in another place. They form a layer.

Metamorphic
- Some igneous and sedimentary rocks may be buried.
- This change makes metamorphic rocks.
- Heat and pressure change these rocks.

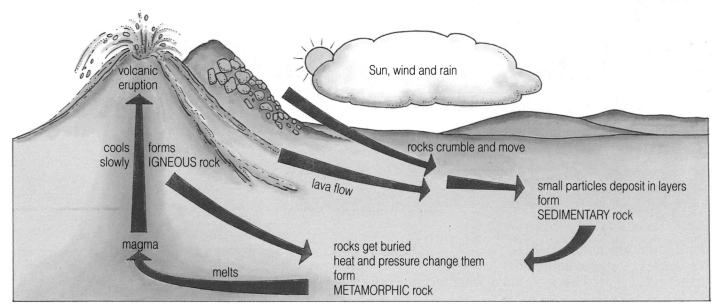

volcanic eruption

Sun, wind and rain

cools slowly | forms IGNEOUS rock

rocks crumble and move

lava flow

small particles deposit in layers form SEDIMENTARY rock

magma

melts

rocks get buried heat and pressure change them form METAMORPHIC rock

c This is called the **rock cycle**. Why do you think this is**?**

Build your own shelter

Investigate rocks for building a shelter.
Which rock is best**?**
What properties does the rock need to have**?**

Plan an investigation.
Show your plan to your teacher. Then carry out your investigation.

1 Copy and complete:
a) A . . . . is a single substance.
b) Most rocks are . . . . of minerals.
c) The 3 main types of rock are . . . . , ...
    and . . . .

2 A gem is a precious mineral.
It can be cut and polished.
Then it is used in jewellery.
a) What makes a mineral precious?
b) Name as many gems as you can.

A ruby

3 Imagine that a limestone quarry is opening near you. You are a local newspaper reporter. Write a **balanced** report about the quarry. Explain why the quarry is important.
Write about problems that might arise.

4 Choose one type of rock.
Make a wall poster about the rock.
Explain how the rock forms. Include drawings.
Do you have any photos of examples? If so, include these.

Things to do

Weathering

Have you ever seen a bottle of frozen milk?
Don't leave your milk on the doorstep in winter. You might get a nasty shock.
But what has this to do with rocks? You can get a clue from a picture below!

All rocks slowly crumble away.
The process is called **weathering**.
All the rocks in the pictures are being **weathered**. They are breaking up.

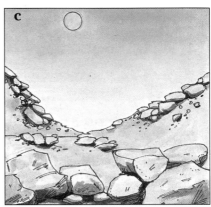

▶ Draw sketches of these pictures. Underneath each write a few lines. Say what you think is causing the weathering.

Rocks under attack

You are provided with samples of:
- limestone rock
- powdered limestone
- sandstone
- powdered sandstone
- dilute acid
- pure water.

⚠ acid
eye protection

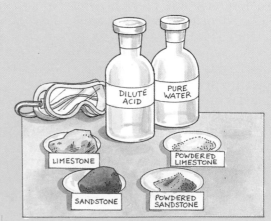

What is the effect of acid rain on rocks?
Plan some investigations.
Show your plans to your teacher.
If it is safe, you can carry out one of your investigations.

Small pieces of rock can get moved from place to place.
Mostly the wind and rivers do this. As the rocks move they
wear away other rocks. This is called **erosion**.
The rock pieces are **transported** to another place.
They are **deposited** in another area.

g What do you think happens next**?**
Remember your rock cycle on page 39.

A break for you or the rocks?

Do you fancy a weekend break**?**
The Jones family owns a hotel in Spotham. It is a lovely old building.
It stands on cliffs overlooking the sea.
But Spotham suffers from coastal erosion.
The sea has been getting closer to the hotel.
Look at the records from 1800:

Date	Distance between hotel and sea in metres
1800	500
1850	410
1875	360
1900	300
1950	200
1975	160

h Plot a graph of these figures.

i Would you like to stay in the hotel**?**

j For how long do you think the hotel can be used**?**

k Can anything be done to help the Jones family**?** How can we
slow down coastal erosion**?**

Things to do

1 Copy and complete. Use the words in the box:

> deposit   erosion
> transported   weathering

Rocks crumble due to . . . .
They are worn away by . . . .
Rock pieces are . . . . to another place.
They . . . . in another area.

2

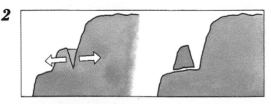

What do you think these diagrams show?
Copy them out. Try to explain this process.

3 Write down the causes of:
a) weathering b) erosion.

4 Make a list of rocks used for building.

5 Coves form when the sea erodes rocks.

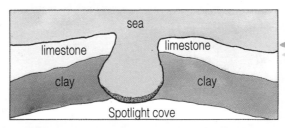

Spotlight cove

Which is the harder rock around the cove?
Limestone or clay?

Explain how you know this.

Elements, mixtures and compounds

How much do you know? Try out these exercises.
Make sure you write down your answers carefully. There's lots to do here!

Find the letters

Do a symbol search. Find the symbols for 8 **metals** in the letters below. The symbols are horizontal or vertical.
Do not mark this book. Write down the symbol. Write the name of the metal next to the symbol.

C	U	M	K	D	C
X	F	E	O	M	Z
S	T	R	N	G	N
N	D	C	A	X	S

Make up your own symbol search for **non-metals**. Hide 6 in the middle of the other letters. Keep a record of your answers.
Let someone else in your group try your symbol search.

Colour me in

Get a copy of the periodic table.
Think about the elements you know.
Colour the metals in blue.
Colour the non-metals in red.

Look for clues

Look at the samples here:

iron   sulphur

a Which are elements?

b Which is the mixture of iron and sulphur?

c Which is the compound?

d How could you get iron from the mixture?

Now 2 very difficult questions:

e How could you get sulphur from the mixture? You must use a different method to **d**!

f What is the compound called?

Try a reaction

eye protection

Fill a test-tube a third full with dilute acid.
Add a 1 cm piece of magnesium ribbon.

Write down what you see.

Can you remember the Reactivity Series?

Think about the zebra in Book 8.

g Which metals react faster than magnesium with acid?

h Which metals are not so reactive with acid?

Copy and complete the word equations.
(Think first. Do they react?)

magnesium + copper sulphate ⟶

magnesium + sodium chloride ⟶

Make it pure

You have 3 solids. One is sulphur. One is salt. One is a mixture of the two.
Your task is to get pure sulphur from the mixture.
You can use any *equipment* you like. But the only chemical allowed is water . . . .

Done it?
Explain how you got the sulphur.
Draw a diagram.

Spot the difference

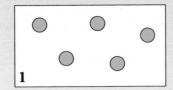

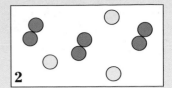

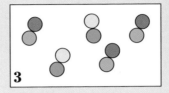

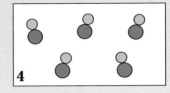

Which of these do you think is:

i an element?

j a mixture of elements?

k a compound?

l a mixture of compounds?

Pick a plate

Sellit Research have made some new compounds.
The compounds are to make plates and cups.
Look at the properties of the compounds.
(A tick means Yes, a cross means No.)

Compound	Can it be moulded?	Does it scratch?	Does it melt below 300°C?	Does it break?	Can it be coloured?	Cost in pence of a 15 cm diameter plate
A	✓	✗	✗	✗	✗	50
B	✓	✓	✗	✗	✓	15
C	✓	✗	✓ at 150°C	✗	✓	15
D	✓	✗	✗	✓	✗	8
E	✓	✗	✗	✓	✓	10

Discuss these compounds in your group.
Which one do you think is best to use? Why?

*Yes, I know it leaks.
. . . but it has got real style*

Things to do

1 Copy and complete. Use the words in the box:

| elements | metals | compounds |
| reactive | unreactive | non-metals |

a) Pure substances are . . . . or . . . .
b) Elements can be . . . . or . . . .
c) Some metals are . . . . e.g. Mg.
d) Some metals are . . . . e.g. Cu.

2 Imagine you have discovered a new element. Describe 4 tests you could do to see if it is a metal or a non-metal.

3 Predict if a reaction will take place:
a) copper + magnesium oxide
b) zinc + potassium chloride
c) zinc + copper sulphate.

Write word equations for the reactions.

Questions

1

In the outline of the periodic table, the numbers represent elements.
Give the numbers of:
a) 3 elements in the same period
b) 3 elements in the same group
c) 2 metals with similar properties
d) 2 non-metals with similar properties.

2 Why **don't** we:
a) use sodium to build cars?
b) use copper to make roads?
c) use silver to make bridges?

3 This is a chromatogram of black ink:
Explain how the chromatogram is made.

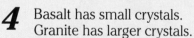

4 Basalt has small crystals.
Granite has larger crystals.
a) Which formed from magma?
b) Which formed from lava?
Explain your answers.

5 Sea defences can be used to limit coastal erosion.
Concrete can be used to build them.
Concrete is made from sand, cement and gravel mixed with water.
Plan an investigation to test different concrete mixes.
Which will make the best sea defence?
You must be able to do your tests in the lab.

6 How can you put metals in order of reactivity?
Write about some tests you could do.

Some metals are very reactive.

The active body

Top sportsmen and sportswomen train hard to develop their strength and stamina.
They also need balance, quick reactions, agility and speed. These are important to all of us, however fit we are.

In this topic you will look at the important systems that make up your active body.

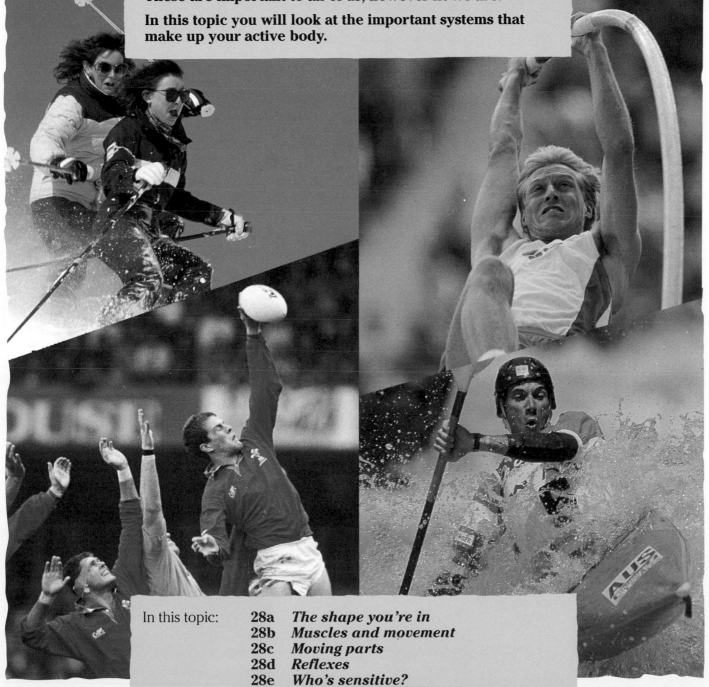

In this topic:

28a | The shape you're in

"I may be bony, but where would you be without me?"

What keeps you in shape? In a word – **bones**.
But not all animals have bones.

a Can you name 3 animals that don't have any bones at all?

Larger animals need lots of bones to keep them in shape.
They need a **skeleton**.

b Write down some ways in which your skeleton helps you.

▶ Your teacher can give you a Help Sheet to find the bones
in your body.
But you don't have to find them all – there are over 200!
Without your skeleton, you would feel really let down!

Protection racket

The bones of your skeleton protect important organs in your body.

c Which part of your skeleton protects your brain?
d Which organs are protected by your ribs?

A great supporting act

Your main supporting bones are shaped like tubes.

- Balance a straw between 2 clamp stands.
- Measure the length of your straw.
- Hang a weight holder from the middle of your straw.
- Carefully add slotted weights until the straw collapses.
- Record the weight needed to bend the straw.
- Now repeat the test with half-length and quarter-length straws.

How does the length of the straw change its strength?

Joints

▶ Try walking without bending your knees, keeping your legs
quite straight.
It's not very easy is it?
So how do you think we move our bones?
Bones can move at **joints**.

Look at these different types of joints:

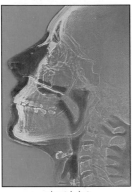
pivot joint

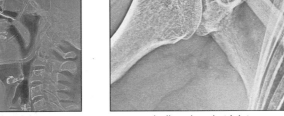
ball and socket joint

hinge joint

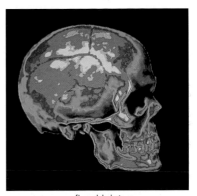
fixed joint

Where do you think they are found in your body?
What type of movement can you make at these joints?

▶ Copy and complete this table with your answers:

Type of joint	Where found	Type of movement
pivot	neck	nodding or turning
ball and socket		
hinge		
fixed		

---

1 Copy and complete:
The . . . . in your skeleton protect many
important . . . . in your body.
Bones also allow . . . . to occur at joints.
Your elbow is an example of a . . . . joint and
your shoulder is an example of a . . . . and
. . . . joint. Many bones are shaped like a
tube. This is a good shape to . . . . your
body.

2 Use your Help Sheet to find:
a) the largest bone in your body, and
b) the smallest, bone in your body.
On your Help Sheet:
c) label as many bones as you can, and
d) shade in red the bones that protect
important organs.

3 Find out as much as you can about what
these do:
a) **tendons** b) **ligaments** c) **cartilage**.

4 As we get older our joints don't work as
smoothly.
There is more friction between the bones at
a joint.
Arthritis can make things worse and so
walking can become very difficult.
Some people have operations to replace
their hip joints with artificial ones.
But the artificial hip joint must have the
same properties as the natural one.
Write down what you think these properties
are.

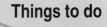
Things to do

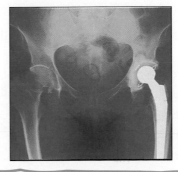

28b Muscles and movement

Are you as muscular as the woman in the photograph? Probably not. But you still have over 350 muscles that do important jobs.

a How do you think the body-builder has developed such powerful muscles?

Your muscles provide the force needed to move bones at **joints**.

▶ Feel your calf muscle at the back of your leg.
Now lift your heel but keep your toes on the floor.
Can you feel your muscle pulling?

No pushing!

Muscles cannot **push** – they can only **pull**.

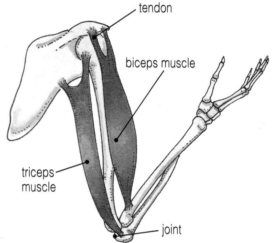

Push up against the underside of the bench with the front of your hand.
b What does your **biceps muscle** feel like?
When it pulls it gets shorter and fatter – we say that it **contracts**.

Now push down with the back of your hand against the bench-top.
c What does your **triceps muscle** feel like?
Your triceps contracts to pull your arm straight.

When a muscle is not contracting, it returns to normal size.
We say that it **relaxes**.

Muscles like your biceps and triceps work in pairs.
When one contracts the other relaxes.
We say that they are **antagonistic**.

▶ Fill in the table to show which muscle contracts and which relaxes:

	Biceps muscle	Triceps muscle
Pushing up with the front of your hand		
Pushing down with the back of your hand		

Muscles at work

The pictures show how a sprinter's leg muscles work at the start of a race.

▶ Look carefully at each picture and find out:
d Which muscle **bends** the knee.
e Which muscle **straightens** the knee.
f Which muscle **bends** the ankle.
g Which muscle **straightens** the ankle.

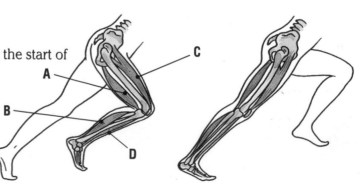

Mighty movers

You can test your finger strength in this investigation.

* Arrange the clamp stand as shown.
* Place your hand flat on the table.
* Put your middle finger through the rubber band.
* Now move your finger down to touch the table.
* Count the number of these finger movements you can do continuously for 2 minutes.
  Be sure to touch the table each time and keep your hand flat.
* Record the number of finger movements for each 20-second period in a table like this:

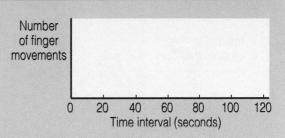

Time interval (seconds)	0–20	20–40	40–60	60–80	80–100	100–120
Number of finger movements						

h Plot a line-graph with axes like this:

i What sort of pattern was there to your results?

j Try to explain any pattern that you observed.

Number of finger movements

0   20   40   60   80   100   120
Time interval (seconds)

---

1 Copy and complete:
Your . . . . provide the force to move . . . . at joints.
A muscle cannot . . . . ; it can only . . . .
When a muscle pulls it gets . . . . and fat.
We say that it . . . . .
When a muscle is not contracting we say that it . . . .

2 Plan an investigation to find out whether exercise or diet is more important in increasing muscle size.

3 Make a model of an arm using your Help Sheet.
Glue the sheet onto cardboard and cut out the shapes of the bones. Join them together with a paper fastener. Use elastic bands for the muscles.
How much weight will your model support? Try to evaluate how much your model works like the real thing.

Things to do

Moving parts

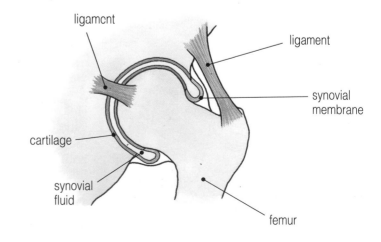

Do you remember learning about **levers** in Book 7?
A lever is a simple **machine**.

Here is a lever being used to lift a sack:
The man is applying an **effort** force to turn the lever and lift the load.
In this case: **a** what is the **load?**
           b where is the **pivot?**
You can draw a simple diagram of the lever like this:

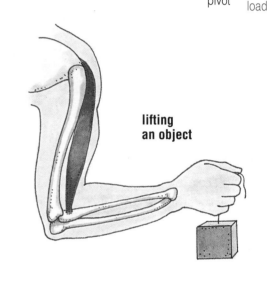

Human moves

Many of your bones work like levers.
Here are 3 levers found in the human skeleton.

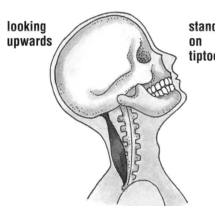

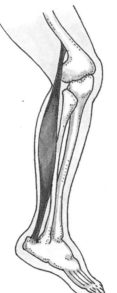

▶ For each one, write down:
  • where the pivot is,
  • where the effort force is applied,
  • where the load is.
  You could make a simple drawing of each one.

Reducing the friction

Your bones move a lot at **synovial joints**.
At these joints, there are tough **ligaments**.
The ends of the bones have a layer of **cartilage**.
Synovial fluid covers the surface of the cartilage.

▶ Look at this diagram of the hip joint:

Which part of this synovial joint do you think:

c holds the bones together?
d reduces friction?
e holds the synovial fluid in place?
f acts as a shock absorber?

Taking the strain

Carry out the four trials of strength in the pictures.
Get your partner to read the scales and record your results.

1

Put the scales on the bench.
Push down with your fists as hard as you can .

2

Put the scales under the edge of the bench.
Push upwards with your hands, as hard as you can.

3

Try squeezing the scales with your fingers.

4

Hold the scales between your two palms.
Push them together as hard as you can.

g Try to identify the muscles that you were using for each test.

h Which muscles do you think produced most force?

i Draw a simple diagram of the levers being used in the first two tests.

Things to do

1 Copy and complete:
Bones which are moved by muscles are working like . . . .
Your bones move a lot at . . . . joints. At these joints, tough . . . . hold the bones together.
The ends of the bones have a layer of . . . . which acts as a . . . . absorber at the joint.
Synovial . . . . reduces . . . . at a joint.

2 How strong is your arm? Plan an investigation different from those above.
(Hint: you may want to use a force-meter.)
You **must** show your plan to your teacher before you try it out.

3 Tendons hold muscles to bones at joints.
Why do you think it is important that a tendon does not stretch when a muscle contracts?

4 Sports injuries often affect muscles and bones.
How do you think each of these sports injuries could happen?
a) Injured tendon (often called a pulled muscle).
b) Bone fracture.
c) Dislocated shoulder.
In which sports would each of these injuries be more likely to happen?

Reflexes

What happens if you accidently touch a hot iron?
If you have any sense, you move away!

a How quickly do you move away?

b Why do you think that you move away quickly?

c How do you think that this happens?

You pull your hand away so quickly because messages are sent around your nervous system at high speed. These tell you what is happening and what to do. This is an automatic action because you do it without thinking.
An *automatic* action like this is called a **reflex**.

Looking at your reflexes

Get your partner to help you investigate your reflexes:

 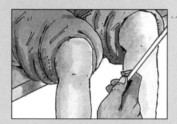  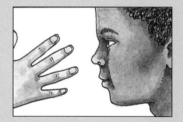

Your partner shines a torch in your eye.
What happens?

Sit on the bench with your legs relaxed.
Your partner taps gently just below your knee.
What happens?

Kneel on a chair and let your feet hang loose.
Your partner taps the back of your foot, just above the heel.
What happens?

Look straight ahead.
Your partner suddenly waves a hand in front of your eyes.
What happens?

d Choose one of these reflexes and say why it is useful to humans?

e What other reflexes do you know?
How are they useful?

Messages

You know that muscles move parts of your body.
But your muscles have to be **told** when and how to work.
Your muscles are controlled by messages that travel along **nerves**.

▶ Look at the diagram:

f What is it that detects the heat of the iron?

g Our skin is a **sense organ**.
Do you know any other sense organs in your body?

h What do you think happens when the messages reach the brain and spinal cord?

i What happens when the messages reach the muscle?

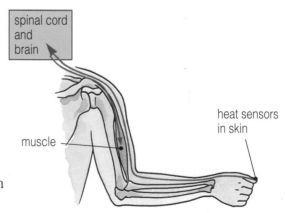

spinal cord and brain

muscle

heat sensors in skin

There's a catch

How fast are your reactions?
Do you think they speed up with practice?

You can measure your reaction time with a falling ruler, as shown in the diagram:

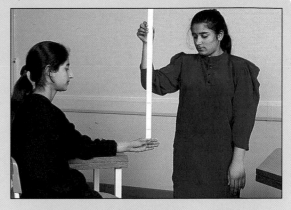

- First add a time scale to the ruler.
  Your teacher will give you a Help Sheet for this.

- Then place your arm on the bench as shown:

  Your partner holds the ruler with the zero next to your little finger, but **not** touching it.
  When your partner lets go of the ruler, try to catch it as quickly as possible.
  Read the scale next to your little finger.
  This shows how long you took.

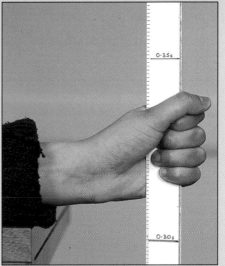

- Now repeat this test 10 times.
  You can record your times in a table like this:

Trial	Time (seconds)	
	Ruler not touching hand	Ruler touching hand
1		
2		

- Now do it another 10 times, but with the ruler now just **touching** your hand.

j What happened to your reaction time with practice?

k Was your reaction time quicker with or without the ruler touching your hand?
Why do you think this is?

l Which of your sense organs were you using?

m Can you change the test so that you use only your hearing?

---

1 Copy and complete:
Sense . . . . in our bodies sends messages at . . . . speed through our . . . .
The messages get our . . . . to move our bodies.
When our nerves work in this way it is called a . . . . action.
Our reflexes are automatic. They work very . . . . and often . . . . us from harm.

2 a) What is meant by your reaction time?
b) Name 3 sports in which you think that reaction time is:
i) important   ii) not important.
c) If you were a tennis player, how could you try to improve your reaction time?

3 Which animals have quick reflexes?
Give some examples of situations where animals need quick reactions in nature.

4 How do you think each of the following can affect a person's reaction time:
a) tiredness? b) coffee (caffeine)?
c) alcohol? d) practice?

Things to do

28e Who's sensitive?

Your skin covers the whole of the outside of your body.
There's about 2 square metres of it.
It acts as a **barrier** between your insides and the air outside.
Write down how you think your skin helps you.

Skin structure

▶ Look at the picture of part of your skin magnified:

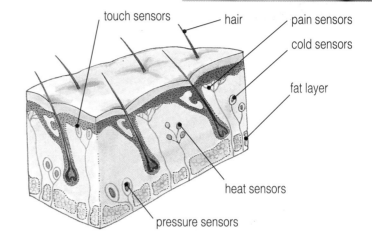

touch sensors   hair   pain sensors
cold sensors
fat layer
heat sensors
pressure sensors

a What sort of things is your skin sensitive to?
What can it feel?

b What do you think the hairs are for?

c Why do you think the fat layer is important?

Test the water

Put one hand into a bowl of iced water and the other into a bowl of warm water.
Keep them there for 1 minute.
Now put both hands into a bowl of water at room temperature.

d What did each hand **feel** like when you took it out of the first bowl?

e What did each hand **look** like when you took it out of the first bowl?

f How did each hand **feel** when you put it into the second bowl?
Try to explain your observations.

Raising a sweat

Andy has just had a hard game of squash.
He looks sweaty and his face is flushed.

g Why do you think that he sweats after he exercises?

He looks flushed because more blood gets to the surface of his skin.

h Why do you think this happens?

i Andy gets changed and goes out into the cold winter weather.
How do you think his skin changes?

j Why do you think this happens?

Get the point?

Your skin contains lots of tiny **touch sensors**.
Which parts of your hand and arm are most sensitive to touch?

- Bend a hair-pin until the points are 5 mm apart.
- Blindfold your partner.
- Gently touch your partner's fore-arm with either 1 or 2 points of the hair-pin.
  Your partner has to say whether they can feel 1 point or 2 points.
- Now repeat this 5 times choosing either 1 point or 2 points each time.
- Record the number of correct choices with a tick in a table like the one below.
- Repeat, this time touching the back of your partner's hand and then their fingertip.
- Now bend the hair-pin to 2 cm apart and repeat the whole exercise again.

Part of body	Hair-pin 5 mm apart	Hair-pin 2 cm apart
Fore-arm		
Back of hand		
Fingertip		

k Which part of your skin do you think was: • most sensitive?
                                                 • least sensitive?

l What does this tell you about the number of touch sensors in each part?

m Plan an investigation to find out which part of your hand and arm is most sensitive to temperature.
Show your plan to your teacher, and then try it out.

1

A	B	C	D	E	F	G	H	I	J	K	L	M

N	O	P	Q	R	S	T	U	V	W	X	Y	Z

Blind people are able to read by using **Braille**.
Each letter of the alphabet is shown by a pattern of 6 dots.
Can you work out what this says?

2 a) What are the 5 senses?
b) If you were riding on a bus, which of these 5 senses would let you know that you were moving?

3 Copy and complete:
Your skin acts as a barrier. It prevents the loss of . . . . by evaporation. It also stops harmful . . . . from entering your body. The hairs and the . . . . layer insulate the skin and reduce the amount of . . . . lost. Sensors in your skin are sensitive to . . . . , pressure and . . . .

4 Find out as much as you can about the following:
a) skin grafts
b) a chemical in the skin called **melanin**
c) finger-prints.

Things to do

Keeping in control

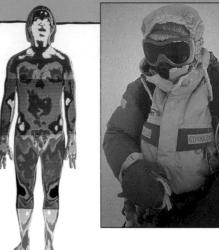

Keeping warm

▶ Look at the thermal image photograph:
It shows which areas of the body give out most energy.

a Which parts of your body lose energy most easily?

b How does the mountaineer in the photograph cut down this heat energy loss?

Air is a good **insulator**.

c How is the mountaineer's clothing designed to trap air?

d The best types of sleeping bag are made out of duck-down. Why do you think that this is better than synthetic fibres?

Body size and cooling

Do small animals lose heat energy more quickly than large animals?

- Half fill a 250 cm³ beaker and a 100 cm³ beaker with hot water.
- Draw a table to record your results.
- Record any changes in temperature in the 2 beakers over the next 15 minutes.
- Plot your results on graph paper.

e Which beaker lost energy more quickly?

f Why do you think this was?

g How could you improve this experiment to make it more accurate?

h Who do you think would lose heat energy more quickly in cold weather, a baby or an adult?

250 cm³
beaker

100 cm³
beaker

stop-clock

Which do you think gives better insulation: fur or feathers?
Plan an investigation to find out.

Keeping your cool

On hot days a lot of heat energy escapes from your body by **sweating**.
As the sweat dries, it takes heat energy from your skin.

▶ Look carefully at the graph:

i At what temperature is the amount of sweat and urine the same?

j If the temperature rises, what happens to the amount of sweat produced? Explain the reason for this.

k If the temperature rises, what happens to the amount of urine produced? Explain the reason for this.

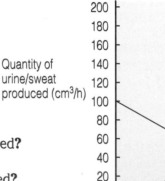

Quantity of urine/sweat produced (cm³/h)

Outside temperature (°C)

Controlling body water

The amount of water in your body is controlled by your **kidneys**.
If you have any extra water in your body, your blood takes it to your kidneys.
The kidneys take the extra water out of the blood to make **urine**.

l Where in your body are your kidneys?

m Where do you think your urine is stored before it leaves your body?

n How does your urine get from your kidneys to your **bladder**?

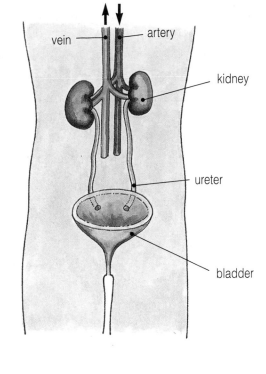

Our kidneys also filter chemical waste out of our bodies.
Most of this waste is in the form of **urea**.

▶ Look at the table:

	Blood concentration (g/l)	Urine concentration (g/l)
Water	900	950
Protein	70	0
Glucose	0.3	0
Urea	3.0	20

o Explain the difference in the amounts of urea in the blood and in the urine.

p Explain the differences in i) the amounts of glucose
       and ii) the amounts of protein.

q What could cause the volume of water in the urine to i) increase?
                                                            ii) decrease?

---

1 Copy and complete:
Our average body temperature is . . . .°C. On hot days we lose . . . . and so keep our body temperature . . . . Also more . . . . gets to the surface of our . . . . to lose heat energy.
Small animals cool . . . . more quickly than larger animals. Our . . . . control the amount of water in our . . . . They also get rid of . . . . chemicals like urea.

2 A **dialysis machine** is used to treat patients with kidneys that are not working properly. Copy this simple diagram and use it to explain how chemical waste, like urea, is removed from a patient's blood.

3 When our body temperature falls below 35°C, we get **hypothermia**.
Which types of people do you think are most at risk from hypothermia?
Explain how the following are important in preventing hypothermia:
a) type of clothing b) a hot meal c) heating.

4 Find out what you can about **Donor Cards**.
Write some points a) in favour of, and b) against, the use of Donor Cards.

Things to do

Donor Card
I would like to help someone to live after my death.

I request that after my death
* A. my *kidneys, *corneas, *heart, *lungs, *liver, *pancreas be used for transplantation, or
* B. any part of my body be used for the treatment of others
                                            *(DELETE AS APPROPRIATE)
Signature _____
Full name _____ Date _____
(BLOCK CAPITALS)
In the event of my death, if possible contact:
Name _____
                    Tel. _____

dialysis fluid in here

dialysis fluid

blood minus waste products

blood and waste products

dialysis membrane

dialysis fluid and waste products out

Questions

1 Many sports injuries affect muscles and bones.
Use a first aid book to find out as much as you can about:
a) fractures b) torn muscles c) dislocations.
Which sports do you think are more likely to cause each type of injury?

2 Devise a programme of exercise to develop:
a) the biceps,
b) the triceps, and
c) the pectoral muscles.

3 a) What joins muscles to bones?
b) What joins bones to bones?
c) What cuts down friction at a joint?
d) What is arthritis?

4 A young child runs out into the road from between 2 parked cars.
A car driver reacts very quickly by slamming on the brakes.
The car screeches to a halt. Luckily the child is unhurt.
Explain, as fully as you can, the way in which the driver's nervous system worked.

5 Can you explain the following?
a) On a cold day, birds like thrushes fluff their feathers up.
b) Several thin layers of clothing keep you warmer than one thick layer.
c) In hot weather, you make small amounts of concentrated urine.

6 How does your body a) gain water? b) lose water?
How does your body control the amount of water loss c) on a hot day?
and d) on a cold day?

7 Why do you think that small animals lose heat energy more easily than large animals?
Small animals, like mice and shrews, have to spend a lot of time eating. Why do you think this is?

Sight and Sound 29

We use our eyes and ears all the time.

We need them to make sense of the world around us.

Light waves and sound waves are useful to us in many other ways as well, as you will see and hear . . .

Reflection and refraction

▶ Kate is looking into a **plane** mirror.
A ray of light from the lamp is ***reflected*** from the mirror:

a Which is the incident ray**?** Which is the reflected ray**?**

b If the angle of incidence is 20°, how big is the angle of reflection**?**

c Explain why Kate sees the lamp.

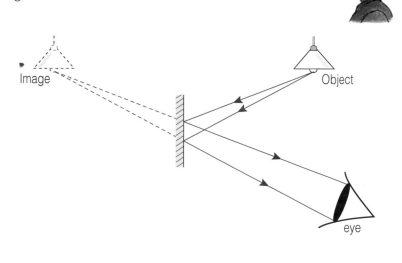

▶ Kate sees an **image** of the lamp. It is called a
virtual image – you cannot touch a virtual image.

d Write down the word IMAGE as it
would look when seen in a mirror.

▶ Here is another diagram of Kate looking at
the lamp:

It shows 2 rays from the lamp going into
Kate's eye.
When Kate looks at the mirror, she sees
the image **behind** the mirror.
The image is ***where the rays appear to
come from***.

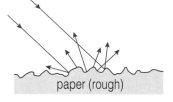

e If the lamp is 2 metres from the mirror,
where exactly does Kate see the image**?**

▶ This diagram shows a beam of light being
scattered from a piece of paper:

f Why can't you see an image in a sheet of
paper**?**

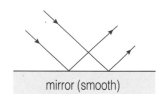

paper (rough)   mirror (smooth)

MIRROR ᴙOᴙᴙIM

Your teacher may give you a Help Sheet with these diagrams:

Tina likes to go to pop concerts, but often she can't see
over the crowd.
How can she use mirrors to see the band?

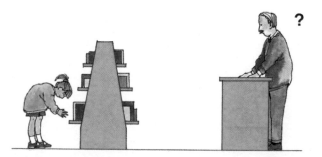

Mr Brown wants to see all the shelves in his shop,
in case of shop-lifters.
How can he use a mirror (or 2 mirrors) to see his shelves?

Refraction

▶ The diagram shows a ray of light going into a glass block:

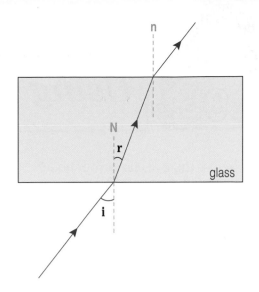

g What happens to the ray when it enters the glass?
This is called **refraction**.
On the diagram you can see a blue dotted line labelled **N**.
This is called the **Normal** line.

h Is the light ray bent away from or towards the normal?

i Which is bigger – the angle of incidence (**i**) or the angle of refraction (**r**)?

Light travels very fast in air – at 300 000 km per second!
In glass it travels more slowly. As the light is slowed down, it is refracted towards the normal.

j What happens to the light ray as it leaves the glass?

Lenses

▶ The diagram shows 2 lenses:

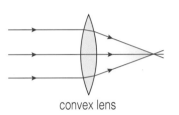

convex lens

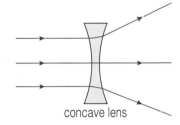

concave lens

k One of them is a **converging** lens and one is a **diverging** lens. Which is which?

Investigating lenses

Your teacher will give you 3 convex lenses (thick, medium, and thin).

- Use each lens as a magnifying glass to look at your finger:

- Which lens magnifies the most? Which least? Is there a pattern?

- What happens if you use 2 lenses together?

- Use them to look at a photo in this book. What do you see?

---

1 Copy and complete:
a) When light is reflected, the angle of .... is .... to the angle of ....
b) The distance from an object to a plane mirror is .... to the distance from the .... to the mirror.
c) When light goes into glass, it is .... towards the normal line.
When light comes out of glass, it is refracted .... from the normal.
d) In a convex lens, the .... come closer together. It is a .... lens.
e) A concave lens is a .... lens.
f) A fat convex lens is a strong .... glass.

2 Think about all the ways that mirrors are used – in homes, shops, and cars. Make a list of all the uses that you can think of, in 2 columns: (1) plane mirrors, (2) curved mirrors.

3 Dave's imagic trick. (Try it!)
The diagram shows Amy looking at a cup:
She cannot see the coin lying in the cup.
Dave pours some water into the cup. Now Amy can see the coin!
Why? Can you explain it by drawing a ray diagram?

Things to do

Using light

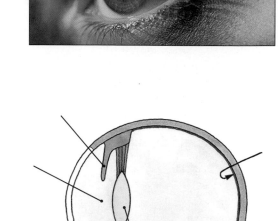

▶ Where is there a lens in your body?
Is it convex or concave?
Does it converge or diverge rays of light?

▶ Sketch a simple diagram of an eye, like the one shown
(or your teacher may give you a Help Sheet).
Then add these labels in the right places:

> **lens   retina   iris   pupil   cornea**

a You are using your eyes to see this page.
Explain, step by step, how the light travels from the
window until it is focussed on your retina.
You can start like this:

Light from the window shines on the book, and then...

b What happens to the pupil in your eye if you look at a
bright light?

Focussing your eyes

The lens in your eye can change shape. When you look at
near objects it gets fatter. For far objects it gets thinner.
The muscles in your eye make the lens go fatter or thinner,
until the image is sharp:

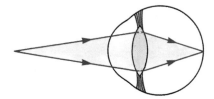

Looking at a near object, your lens is *fat*.

If you can't see a near object clearly, you are long-sighted.
(You may need spectacles with con<u>vex</u> lenses.)

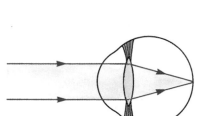

Looking at a far object, your lens is *thin*.

If you can't see a distant object clearly, you are short-sighted.
(You may need spectacles with con<u>cave</u> lenses.)

Eye tests

Plan, and carry out, an investigation to find out the distances
at which you can read letters of different sizes.

• How will you make it a fair test?

• Is it the same for the left eye, the right eye, and both eyes?

• Plot a graph of the **distance from your eye** against the
size of the letter. What do you find?

• Is your graph the same as other people's?

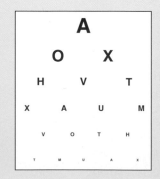

A	4 mm
O X	3 mm
H V T	2 mm
X A U M	1.5 mm
v o t h	1 mm
T M U A X	0.6 mm

size of letters

The camera

In a camera, a lens is used to make an image on the film:

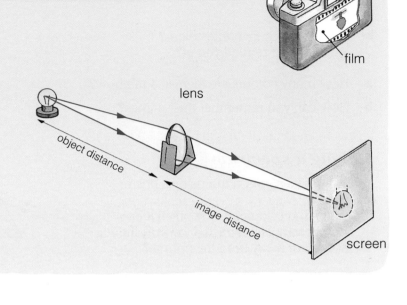

Use a convex lens to focus the light rays from a lamp, like in a camera:

- What do you notice about the image?
- Move the lamp to different distances from the screen. Each time, focus the image. Measure the distances shown on the diagram, and record them in a table.
- What pattern do you find?

- In a camera, how do you focus on
  - near objects?
  - far objects?

- Does your eye focus on objects in this way?

▶ Look at this diagram of a camera:

c Which part of the camera is like your retina?

The **aperture** can be changed to let in more or less light.

 open closed

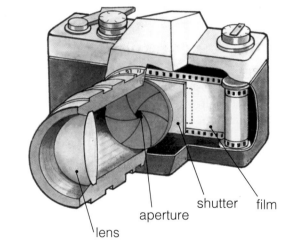

d Which part of your eye is like this?

e When should the camera use a small aperture?

f In what other way can a camera change the amount of light going to the film?

g The camera and your eye both use a lens. In what ways are the lenses i) similar? and ii) different?

h Explain carefully how your eye and a camera use different ways to focus the image.

---

1 Copy and complete:
a) My eye lens is a . . . . lens. It . . . . the rays of light.
b) To focus on near and far objects, my eye . . . . changes shape. To focus on . . . . objects, it is fatter.
c) A long-sighted person cannot focus on . . . . objects. A short-sighted person cannot focus on . . . . objects.
d) The . . . . in a camera and in my eye are inverted (upside-down).

2 Copy and complete:
a) A camera uses a . . . . lens.
b) To focus a camera on near objects, the lens is moved . . . . from the film.
c) The . . . . in a camera is like the iris in my eye.

3 Draw up a table or a poster which shows all the ways in which a camera and your eye are i) similar, and
ii) different.

Things to do

A world of colour

▶ Which is your favourite colour?
What does it remind you of?

a How many colours are there in a rainbow?

b How can you remember their names?

Making a spectrum

You can make a **spectrum** using a prism:

c When the light enters the prism it is
refracted. Is it refracted towards the
normal or away from the normal?

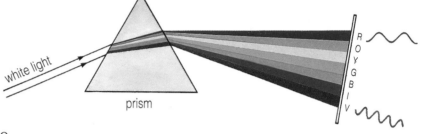

white light

prism

The white light is **dispersed** by the prism, to
make a spectrum.
This shows that white light is really a mixture
of seven colours.

d Write down the full names of the 7 colours,
in order.

e Red light has the longest wavelength.
Which colour has the shortest?

The light is refracted because it travels slower
in the glass than in the air.
Different colours travel at different speeds, and
so are refracted by different amounts.

f Which colour do you think travels slowest
in glass?

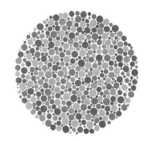

Can you see a red number here?
If you can't, you may be colour-blind.

Filters

What do you see when you look through a piece of red
plastic or red glass?
A red **filter** will only let through red light:
It **absorbs** all the other colours:

g Which colour passes through a green filter?

h Which colours are absorbed by a green filter?

i Use this diagram to explain what you see when you
look through a blue filter and a red filter together:

j Where have you seen filters used?

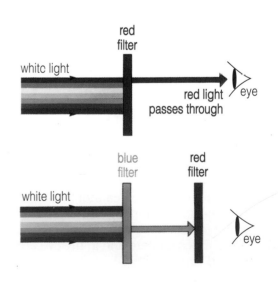

red
filter

white light

red light
passes through

eye

blue
filter

red
filter

white light

eye

Seeing coloured objects

k The paper in this book looks white.
Write down which colours you think are being reflected from it.

l Use the diagram to explain what happens when white light shines on green paper:

m Explain what is happening when you look at this red ink

Green things reflect green light and absorb the other colours. We see the green light.

Designing for the stage

Imagine you are the stage-designer for a pop group.
You have to design the band's clothes as well as the stage colours. The manager tells you that the stage lights will flash red or green or blue.
The picture shows someone's first attempt:

- Look at this picture in red light, in green light, and in blue light. (Or look through filters.)

- Draw up a table to show what colours a white, a red, a green and a blue object look like in white, red, green and blue lights.

- Then re-design the set and the clothes so that the band can be seen better.

Safety first

Plan an investigation to see which is the safest colour for you to wear when riding a bicycle, or walking on a road.

- How will you make it a fair test?

- How will you find out which is the safest colour for both day-time and night-time?

- Show your plan to your teacher and, if you have time, do it.

- How else can you improve your safety on the road?

Things to do

1 Copy and complete:
a) White light is .... by a prism into a spectrum. The 7 colours are:
b) .... light has the longest wavelength.
c) The colour refracted the most is ....
d) A red filter lets .... light through, and .... all the other colours.
e) A blue T-shirt reflects .... light, and .... all the other colours.

2 What colour would a red book look:
a) in red light?   c) through a red filter?
b) in green light? d) through a blue filter?

3 Which jobs may be dangerous if you are colour-blind?

4 Plan an investigation to see which colours are best for an easy-to-read disco poster.

Musical sounds

▶ Touch the front of your throat while you say 'aaah'.
Can you feel it **vibrating**?

a Explain, step by step, how someone else can hear this sound.

b What is vibrating in 1) a guitar?
2) a drum?
3) the recorder in the photo?

Waves on a spring

You can use a 'slinky' spring to 'model' a sound wave.
When you vibrate the end, a wave of energy travels down the spring:

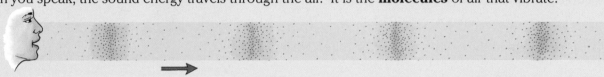

wavelength

energy

This kind of wave is called a **longitudinal** wave.

When you speak, the sound energy travels through the air. It is the **molecules** of air that vibrate:

The energy is transferred from molecule to molecule. They vibrate like the coils of the spring.

c Why can't sound travel through a vacuum?

An oscilloscope

You can use a **c**athode **r**ay **o**scilloscope (**CRO**) to
investigate sound waves.

The sound energy enters the microphone. The energy is
transferred to electrical energy, which goes to the oscilloscope.
A **wave** is shown on the screen.

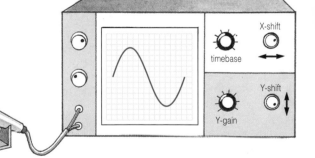

What happens if you 1) turn the Y-shift knob?
2) turn the X-shift knob?
3) switch the time-base off and on?
4) change the Y-gain dial?

Loudness and amplitude

• Hum or whistle a quiet sound into the microphone.

• Then do the same sound but **louder**.
How does the wave change?

• Sketch the 2 waves.

• How does the **amplitude** of a wave depend on
the loudness of the sound?

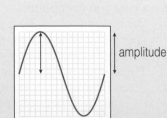

amplitude

Which note is louder?

Pitch and frequency

- Hum or whistle a note with a low pitch, and then a high pitch. How does the wave change?

- Sketch the 2 waves.

- Waves with a shorter wavelength have a higher **frequency**. The molecules are vibrating more often. Frequency is measured in **hertz** (**Hz**). A note of 300 Hz means it is vibrating 300 times in each second.

- How does the pitch of your notes depend on the frequency?

- Blow a dog-whistle. What do you notice? What is ultra-sound?

- Connect a signal-generator to a loudspeaker, to make sound waves of different frequencies. What is the highest note you can hear? Sketch its wave.

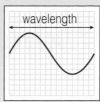

Low frequency

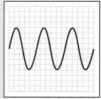

High frequency

Which note is high-pitched?

Musical instruments

- Make different sounds – aaah, ooo, eee – while you watch the screen.

- Play different musical instruments. Play the same note on each one, and sketch the waves.

- In what ways are the waves   1) the same?   2) different?

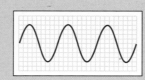

recorder

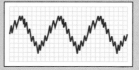

guitar

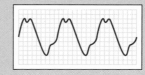

violin

Reflecting a sound

Plan an experiment to see if the angle of incidence is equal to the angle of reflection for a sound wave.

Things to do

1 Copy and complete:
a) A sound . . . . is caused by vibrations. It is a . . . . wave. The energy is transferred from molecule to . . . .
b) A loud sound has a large . . . .
c) A high-pitched sound has a high . . . .
d) Frequency is measured in . . . . (Hz).

2 Write down the names of 10 musical instruments that do not use electricity. For each one, say whether it is plucked, blown, bowed, hit or shaken.

3 Humming birds make a noise by beating their wings very quickly. Plan an investigation to find out the frequency at which their wings vibrate.

4 The diagrams below show 4 waves.
a) Which has the largest amplitude?
b) Which has the highest frequency?
c) Which was the quietest sound?
d) Which sound had the lowest pitch?
e) Which 2 have the same amplitude?
f) Which 2 have the same frequency?

A

B

C

D

Using sound

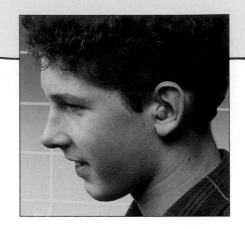

▶ Why do some people wear a hearing aid?
Do you know anyone who wears one?
What do you think is inside a hearing aid?

Your ear can easily be damaged. This causes deafness.
You looked at this in *Spotlight Science 7*.

a In what ways can your ear be damaged?
Write down as much as you can remember about this.

How loud?

If you stand too close to a loudspeaker in a disco, you could damage
your hearing.
Does it matter *where* you stand? Plan an investigation to find out.

• What will you use to detect the sound?

• How will you keep a record of the different positions that you try?

• Predict what you think you will find.

• If you have time, try it.

▶ Joanne sees a lightning flash on a hill which she knows is
1000 metres away. She hears the sound 3 seconds later.

b Which travels faster, sound or light?

c Use the formula:

$$\text{speed} = \frac{\text{distance travelled}}{\text{time taken}}$$

to calculate the speed of sound in air.

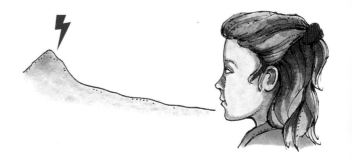

d Sound travels faster in water (a liquid) and even faster in
iron (a solid). Why do you think this is?

Echoes

Sailors can use **echoes** to find the depth of the sea:

▶ Suppose this ship sent out a sound wave, and got back an echo
after 1 second.

e How long did it take for the sound to get down to the bottom?

f How far does the sound travel in this time? (The speed of sound
in water is 1500 metres per second.)

g How deep is the sea?

h If the fish are 250 m deep, what would be their echo time?

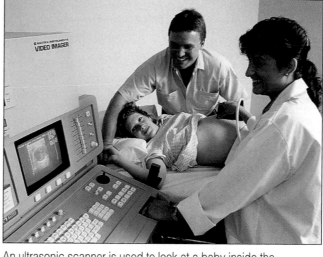

Bats and dolphins use **ultrasound** to find food and 'see' in the dark.

i What is ultrasound?

j How do the bats and dolphins use it?

An ultrasonic scanner is used to look at a baby inside the mother's womb. It works like the echo-sounder on a ship.

k This scanner is not as dangerous as using X-rays. Why do you think this is?

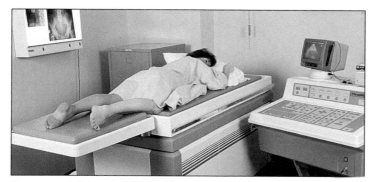

Stones can build up inside your kidneys. They are very painful. Here a high-energy beam of ultrasound is being used to break them into tiny pieces. Then they can come out with the urine.

Opticians can use ultrasound to clean spectacles. Inside the box, the vibrations shake the dirt loose. The same idea can be used to clean dirty clothing.

Geologists use echo-sounding to search for oil and gas:

l In the diagram, which microphone will receive the sound first?

m The speed of sound in rock is about 4000 m/s. If the sound arrives at the microphone after $\frac{1}{2}$ second, estimate the depth of the hard rock layer.

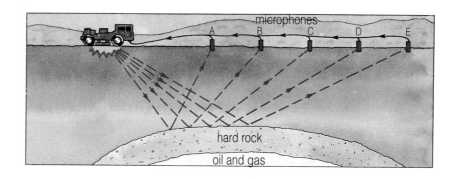

---

1 Copy and complete:
a) Light travels . . . . than sound.
b) The formula for speed is:
c) Sound travels . . . . in iron than in water.
   It travels . . . . in water than in air.
d) When sound is reflected, you get an . . . .
   This is used in . . . . -sounding.
e) Ultrasound has a frequency which is too
   . . . . for us to hear.

2 Make a list of jobs you could not do if your hearing was damaged.

3 If you hear thunder 15 seconds after seeing lightning, how far away is the storm? (Speed of sound = 330 m/s)

4 Do you think background music in shops persuades people to buy more things? Plan an investigation to answer this.

5 School canteens are usually very noisy. How could you make yours quieter? Draw a plan of it and label all the improvements you would make if you were an architect.

Things to do

Questions

1 Suppose you can choose from a variety of mirrors (plane and curved) and lenses (converging and diverging).
Work out a design for each of these:
   a) a torch
   b) a periscope to see at a football match
   c) a periscope to see behind you in a car
   d) a solar cooker
   e) a spy camera to take photos round corners
   f) an over-head projector for a teacher.

Draw a labelled diagram of each design. On each diagram, draw coloured lines to show what happens to the rays of light.

2 Natalya is only 3 years old. She can speak but she can't read yet, so it is hard to use the usual eye-test with her:
Design a test that could be used instead.

3 Some pupils were hypothesizing about the effects of colour.

Anna said, "I think more people choose to eat green jelly than any other colour."
Jamie said, "I think that flies are more likely to land on yellow surfaces than white surfaces."

Choose one of these hypotheses, and plan an investigation to test it. Take care to make it a fair test.

4 John made some notes about electromagnetic waves, but they got mixed up:

   a) One type of wave should not be included at all. Which one?
   b) List the rest of the waves in order of their wavelength.
   c) Next to each one, put the correct comment.

Gamma rays   Infra-red   Sound waves
Gives you a sun-tan. Dangerous   Light waves
Given out by warm objects   Radio waves   Similar to x-rays. Dangerous
Used by your eyes   Used by doctors to see inside your body
X-rays   Ultra-violet   Used to communicate over long distances

5 Kelly says, "There ought to be a law against playing music loudly." Do you agree with her?
Give your arguments for and against this idea.

6 The diagram shows a wave-form on an oscilloscope:
   a) What is the time taken for 1 wave?
   b) How many waves are there in 100 milliseconds?
   c) How many waves will there be in 1 second?
      (1 second = 1000 milliseconds)
   d) What is the frequency of the wave?
   e) Would this be a high note or a low note?

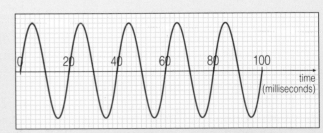

7 The time-keeper of a 100 m race stands at the finishing line. He starts his stop-watch when he hears the starter's pistol.

   a) Will the time he measures be too long or too short?
   b) By how much? (Speed of sound in air = 340 m/s)

70

Health

We all want to have happy, healthy and active lives. But to do so, we need to take good care of our bodies. We should eat the right foods and take regular exercise. We should understand the dangers to our health of alcohol, drugs and solvents.

In this topic you will also find out about disease and how we can fight it.

Are you fit**?**

▶ Write down some of your ideas about what it means to be fit.

Look at the people in the photos:
Each person must be fit to do their sport well.

S-factors

Four things make up fitness:

- **Strength** is the amount of force that your muscles can exert.

a Which exercises do you think could make you stronger**?**
b Which things that you do every day need strength**?**
c Which sports in the photographs need strong muscles**?**

- **Stamina** keeps you going during exercise.
  To develop your stamina, you need a strong heart and lungs.

d Which sports in the photographs need a lot of stamina**?**
e What sort of exercises do you think would improve your stamina**?**
f How can people's life-styles reduce their stamina**?**

- **Suppleness** lets you move freely and easily.
  If you are supple, you can bend, stretch and twist your body easily.

You often see people 'warming up' before they do sport.

g What exercises do they do**?**
h What might happen if they did not do these 'warm up' exercises**?**
i Which sports in the photographs need you to be supple**?**

- **Speed** is having quick reactions or how fast you travel over a distance.

j Which sports in the photographs need speed over a distance**?**
k Which sports in the photographs need quick reaction times**?**
l How can you improve both types of speed**?**

Stretching a point

Charlotte says "I think that girls are always more supple than boys".
Faris does not agree with her.
Plan an investigation to see who is right.
When you have done your plan, show your teacher,
then try it out.

We're getting fitter!

More people are getting exercise from sport or fitness activities.
When you do different activities you need different amounts of your
S-factors.

▶ Look at the table.

Exercise	Strength	Stamina	Suppleness	Speed
Badminton	**	**	***	**
Climbing stairs	**	***	*	*
Cycling (hard)	***	****	**	*
Dancing (disco)	*	***	***	*
Football	***	***	***	***
Golf	*	*	**	*
Gymnastics	***	**	****	**
Hill walking	**	***	*	*
Jogging	**	****	**	*
Swimming	****	****	****	**
Tennis	**	***	***	***
Weight-training	****	*	*	*

*no real effect **good effect ***very good effect ****excellent effect

m Which exercises do you think are best for i) strength ii) stamina
iii) suppleness iv) speed?

n Which exercise do you think is i) best and ii) worst for
your all round fitness?

o Karen is 14. She isn't sporty. What exercises can you suggest to
keep her fit?

Fitness programme

Think up a fitness programme that a year 9 pupil could do in
10 minutes a day. Make a leaflet of your programme.
It should:

- include all four S-factors (strength, stamina, suppleness, speed).
- not involve any special equipment like weights.
- not be too difficult.
- not need a large space to do it in.

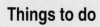

You should not try the programme out unless it has been checked by your teacher.
And remember, if you feel any strain during exercise, stop and rest.

---

1 Copy and complete:
Strength is the amount of . . . . that your . . . .
can exert . . . . . keeps you going when
you exercise hard. If you can bend, twist
and stretch your body easily, then you are
. . . . Speed can mean being fast over a . . . .
or having quick . . . . You need all 4 of these
. . . . to be fit.

2 Think up a fitness programme for
someone who does a) netball b) rowing
c) sprinting.

3 Use the table above to suggest suitable
exercises for these people:
a) a 45-year-old man who has recovered
from a heart attack.
b) a 27-year-old mother who had her first
baby 10 weeks ago.
c) a 50-year-old woman who has never
played sport.

4 Choose one sport that you enjoy and
design a poster to encourage people to take
part in it.

Things to do

30b Healthy growth

How do you think a 3 kg baby gets to be a 75 kg adult?
What do we mean by **growth?**
Write down some of your ideas.

Growth is a permanent increase in size.

Patterns of growth

You can measure your growth in different ways.
You can measure your height, your weight, or the length of things
like your middle finger.

a Why do you think that weight might not be such a useful
measure of growth?

▶ Look at the diagram showing human growth:
For each age, carefully measure in millimetres:

- the length of the head, and
- the length of the body from the neck to the feet.

Record your results in a table.
Draw a graph of your results (with age on the horizontal axi
and length on the vertical axis).

b Can you see any pattern as we get older?

birth	2 years	5 years	15 years	20 years

How tall might you grow?

You can use the chart to estimate how tall you might grow.

▶ Use the formula:

$$\frac{\text{present height (cm)}}{\text{\% of full height}} \times 100 = \text{full height}$$

For example, for a boy aged 12 who is 150 cm tall:

$$\frac{150}{84} \times 100 = 179 \text{ cm}$$

So the boy could be 179 cm when he has stopped growing.

Don't forget that different people have growth spurts at different times.

Age	Percentage of full height	
	Boys	Girls
8	72	78
9	75	81
10	78	84
11	81	88
12	84	93
13	87	97
14	92	98
15	96	99
16	98	100
17	99	100
18	100	100
19	100	100

How do we grow?

I think that when you grow your cells get bigger.

I think that when you grow, you make more new cells.

Who do you think is right?
You can use the photos of human cells as evidence.

from a 5-year-old

from a 20-year-old

We grow when one cell divides to make 2 new cells.

c Draw some simple diagrams to show how you think one cell divides.

d How could one cell eventually make eight?

Lots of clots

For healthy growth you need a balanced diet.
You especially need protein and vitamins for growth.

When you were a baby you got your protein from milk.
The enzyme **rennin** is made in the stomachs of young animals.
It makes milk solid, so that it stays in the stomach longer.
It can then be digested.

Plan an investigation into how quickly rennin clots milk.
Think about the factors that might affect how quickly rennin works.
Choose one factor and investigate its effect.

- How will you make it a *fair test*?
- How will you decide when the milk has clotted?
- How will you record your results?

Show your plan to your teacher before you try it out.

Growth out of control

When cell division gets out of control, a lump or **tumour** can form.
Sometimes the tumour is **malignant**. Some cells may break away
and get into the bloodstream.
This is how **cancer** cells can spread to other parts of the body.
If a cancer is detected early, it is more likely that it can be treated
successfully. Fortunately many people who suffer from cancer now
recover and lead normal healthy lives.

e Find out about treatments for cancer like radiotherapy and
chemotherapy.

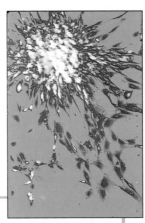

Tumour with
cancer cells
breaking away

Things to do

1 Here is a table which shows Liam's
height since he was born:

Age (years)	birth	2	3	4	5	6	7	8	9	10	11	12	13	14	15	16	17	18
Height (cm)	50	85	95	103	110	115	120	125	130	135	140	145	150	160	170	173	174	175

a) Plot a line-graph to show how Liam's
height has changed.
b) Explain the shape of the graph.
c) During which years was Liam growing
fastest?

2 Copy and complete:
Growth is a permanent . . . . in size. You can
measure growth by looking at the increase in
. . . . , in weight or in length. During growth
. . . . divide and so our bodies increase in size.
For healthy growth we need to have a
balanced . . . . We need lots of . . . . and
vitamins in order to make new cells.
Cancers can occur when cell . . . . gets out of
control. Cancer can be successfully treated
by radiotherapy and by . . . .

3 Here are 3 places in your body where
the cells divide quickly:
a) skin b) bone marrow c) stomach lining.
Why do you think cells grow so quickly in
these places?

4 Your growth is controlled by an organ
called the **pituitary**.
The pituitary is found underneath your brain.
It controls your growth by making
hormones.
Find out what you can about the pituitary.

A drink problem

Alcohol is a **drug**.
In Britain drinking alcohol is **socially acceptable** but people can become **addicted** to it.

a Write down what you think the highlighted words mean.

Most drugs affect the brain and nervous system.
Alcohol is a **depressant** drug.

b What effect do you think alcohol has on the way your body works**?**

Alcohol is made by **fermentation**.

c Can you remember what happens during this process**?**

d Alcohol is sipped and swallowed. But where do you think it goes after that**?**
Your teacher may give you a Help Sheet which shows how alcohol can affect your body.

Units of alcohol

All these drinks contain **1 unit** of alcohol:

After drinking 1 unit of alcohol, the amount of alcohol in the blood increases by 16 mg in 100 cm^3.

▶ Match **e** to **j** with the correct units of alcohol in the pictures.

e The legal limit for driving.

f No obvious effects, but your reactions are slower.

g Speech is slurred, seeing double, feeling emotional, may be tearful or looking for a fight.

h Talkative, your judgement is not so reliable.

i Possible loss of consciousness.

j Feeling more cheerful.

1 unit

12 units

2 units

16 units

3 units

5 units

Dave goes downhill

When Dave started work for a local firm he soon got to know the other lads. He had the odd drink with them at lunchtime even though it made him feel a bit sleepy.

With the money he made, Dave could afford to go down the pub in the evenings as well. Some nights he would stay out so late that he found it difficult to get up for work next morning.

One afternoon Dave made a mistake that could have caused a serious accident at work. As he had been warned about being late many times, this was the last straw – he was sacked!

Out of work and with nothing to do, Dave now needed a drink even more. He became bad-tempered and started to borrow money from friends for a drink.

k What do you think was the cause of: i) Dave's mistake at work?
ii) Dave being late for work?

▶ Look at the graph:

l How many units of alcohol are removed from the blood every hour?

m Dave goes home at 11 p.m. after drinking 10 pints of beer.
How long does it take for all the alcohol to get out of his blood?

n At what time would he be below the legal limit for driving?

Hours needed for alcohol in blood to fall to zero

Units of alcohol

What people say about drinking

I can take or leave alcohol. If there's none around then I'm happy with soft drinks.

I have a good drink with the lads after a rugby match.

My dad was down the pub every night and I'm just like him.

I have a drink at parties. It makes me less shy about talking to people.

I always have a glass of wine with a good meal.

I like a drink after work - it helps me to unwind.

I get lonely on my own. A drink cheers me up a bit.

All my crowd drinks. At weekends we get mental.

In your groups discuss:

• Why you think each person drinks.

• Which people you think are at low risk from alcohol.

• Which people you think could become problem drinkers.

Either Choose to be one of the characters and act out a discussion about the dangers of heavy drinking.

or Choose a character and write a story to show how heavy drinking can cause difficulties in the family.

---

1 Copy and complete:
Alcohol is a . . . . because it affects your . . . . system by . . . . down your reactions. For this reason, people should not drink if they are to . . . . machines or . . . . a car. A pint of beer contains . . . . units of alcohol. The legal limit for driving is . . . . People who drink too much can become . . . . to alcohol.

2 When Louise was 13 she took a friend home at lunchtime. They helped themselves to drinks from her parents' drinks cabinet. Write an ending to the story.

3 What do you think should be done to get rid of the problems caused by alcohol? How successful do you think these would be:
a) pubs opening for longer or shorter times?
b) raising or lowering the age at which it is legal to buy alcohol?
c) making alcoholic drinks more expensive?

Things to do

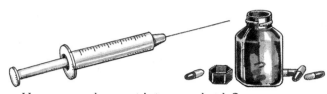

What does the word **drug** mean to you?

Here are some pictures of different drugs.
▶ Use them to help you write about what a drug is.

a How can a drug get into your body?

b Why can it affect **all** of your body?

c How do you think a drug can save lives?

d How many drugs do you know of?
Make a list of them.

e Did you include any of these in your list:
aspirin, coffee, alcohol, cigarettes, insulin, aerosols?
Why do you think that these can be drugs?

Disco girl killed by one tablet of new drug

An 18-year-old girl has died after taking a single tablet of a new designer drug. A court heard yesterday how Linda took the pill to give her energy at an all-night disco. She collapsed on the dance floor and was rushed to hospital screaming in pain. She suffered 2 heart attacks and died from lack of oxygen to the brain 2 days later. Her parents were at her bedside.

The judge branded the drug barons who supply drugs like ecstasy "scum and filth". He imposed 6-month sentences on 3 young people who admitted pushing the drug.

In your groups discuss:

• Why Linda took the drug in the first place.

• How she got hold of the drug.

• What action should be taken, and by who?

In your groups: Talk about situations where teenagers may be offered drugs. What reasons might influence them to accept or refuse?

and Write a script for a short scene showing the dangers of taking drugs. Choose a role and try to speak and act as if you are the person.
Your teacher might choose your group to act your scene to the class.

or Write one or two paragraphs saying why you think teenagers start to take drugs.
Say what your views on drug-taking are.

Solvent abuse

What do you think is meant by **solvent abuse**?

▶ Use your ideas and some of these facts to write a few lines about it.

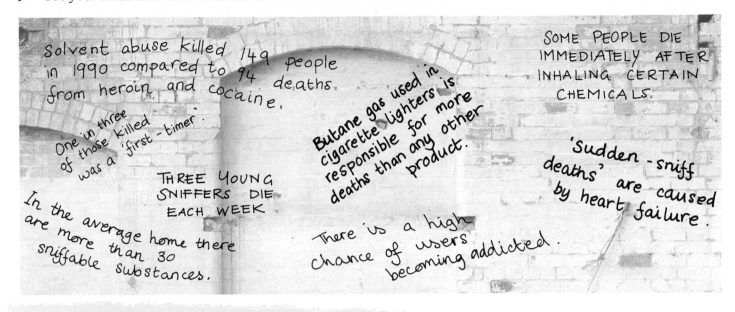

Solvent abuse killed 149 people in 1990 compared to 94 deaths from heroin and cocaine.

One in three of those killed was a 'first-timer'.

In the average home there are more than 30 sniffable substances.

THREE YOUNG SNIFFERS DIE EACH WEEK

Butane gas used in cigarette lighters is responsible for more deaths than any other product.

There is a high chance of users becoming addicted.

SOME PEOPLE DIE IMMEDIATELY AFTER INHALING CERTAIN CHEMICALS.

'Sudden-sniff deaths' are caused by heart failure.

Lingering death of glue-sniffer Carl

A 21-year-old man was found hanged in a garage after 10 years of glue-sniffing.

When he was 11, Carl and some older friends went to a nearby building site and experimented with glue. He said "It was a laugh at the time and all the gang tried it."

His sniffing really started after he moved house and started at secondary school. His mother also had a new baby so he didn't get so much attention. Carl started to truant from school and discovered a gang of sniffers. At 14 he was taken into care – he felt rejected by his family. He shop-lifted to get glue and got into trouble with the police. By 18 he was often aggressive. He drifted from hostels to bedsits and often slept rough. What money he had was used to get more glue.

Carl aged 11 with friends

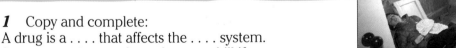

f Why do you think Carl started to sniff glue?

g What events in his life might have made him continue the habit?

h Why do you think that Carl truanted from school?

i How do you think people like Carl could be helped?

1 Copy and complete:
A drug is a . . . . that affects the . . . . system. Some . . . . save . . . . but others can kill if you take an . . . . Some people can't stop taking some drugs because they are . . . . Solvents are . . . . available and can attract . . . . people and those too . . . . to afford other drugs.

2 Explain how each of the following might make a few young people start to take a drug:
a) curiosity b) friends c) self-pity.
What type of person might be influenced most easily?

3 Two teenagers are found by a teacher, in an old house, inhaling solvent.
What happens next? What should the teacher do in the best interests of the teenagers and the school? Write the rest of the story.

4 Design a leaflet which shows some of the signs and symptoms of solvent abuse that shopkeepers could keep by the till.

Things to do

Microbes and disease

Do you know why people get ill**?**

▶ Make a list of some of the things that you think make people ill.

Your skin acts as a barrier to microbes.

a Can you remember the main types of microbes**?**

Bacteria and viruses are a common cause of disease.

b Make a list of some diseases caused by these microbes.

The **symptoms** of a disease are the body's response to waste chemicals made by the microbes.

c Write down some symptoms that you know of.

Points of entry

Look at these ways in which diseases can be spread:

air   food   touch   water   animals

d For each method shown in the picture, write down:
  i) A disease that can be spread in this way (your teacher can give you a Help Sheet).
  ii) How its spread can be prevented.

e Can you think of any other ways in which diseases can be spread**?**

▶ Use your Help Sheet of diseases to find out the answers to the following questions.

f What type of microbe causes i) tuberculosis**?** ii) measles**?** iii) athlete's foot**?**

g What are the symptoms of i) polio**?** ii) mumps**?** iii) the common cold**?**

h How are i) malaria ii) rubella, and iii) athlete's foot spread**?**

Seldomill Health Authority

Memo to: *Analysts*   **From:** *Mike Robe*

The children at Sick Lee High School have been going down with severe stomach upsets. I think that the disease may be linked to places where they eat their lunch. These are the school canteen, the Greasy Cod Chip Shop, Sid's Snack Bar and Betty's Bakery.
Please plan an investigation to find out the source of infection. Write me a report about your plan, the tests you intend to use, and how you will show your results.

Please hurry!

Antibiotics: useful drugs

Your doctor might give you an **antibiotic** to help you fight a disease.
The first antibiotic was discovered by Alexander Fleming.

Just like Fleming!

- Using sterile forceps, place a sterile paper disc into each of:

  A – disinfectant   **B** – alcohol   **C** – crystal violet
  D – washing-up liquid

- Leave to soak for 5 minutes.
- You will be given an agar plate which has harmless bacteria growing on it.
- Divide the underneath of an agar plate into 6 sections and label them **A** to **F**.
- Remove the discs with sterile forceps and shake off any excess liquid.
- Place each disc on the correct part of the agar plate.
- Your teacher will give you a **penicillin** and a **streptomycin** disc for sectors **E** and **F**.
- Sellotape the lid to the base so it cannot come off.
- Incubate your plate for 48 hours at 25°C. Then examine the growth of bacteria.

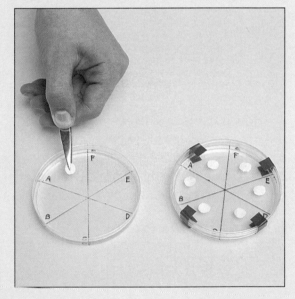

i   Which chemical had most effect upon the growth of the bacteria?

j   How were you able to measure this effect?

k   How could you use this test to find out the best concentration of an antibiotic to use?

---

1   Copy and complete:
Bacteria and . . . . are the main microbes that cause disease. The . . . . of a disease are caused by chemicals made by the microbes. A drug that fights the disease inside your body is called an . . . . Alexander . . . . discovered one of the first antibiotics.

2   Name 4 ways in which diseases can be spread.
For each way say how you think the disease can be prevented.

3   Drugs that kill microbes inside the body are called **antibiotics**.
Find out what **antiseptics** and **disinfectants** are and how they help to fight disease.

4   How do you think the following can help to spread disease:
a) flies?   b) hypodermic needles?
c) kitchen clothes?

Things to do

How is it that our bodies are able to fight off disease? If you catch a disease like measles, you don't get it again – you become **immune**.

Why do you think this happens? Write down your ideas.

▶ Find out which diseases people in your class are immune to.

Jenner vaccinating his son

THE GLOUCESTER TIMES

BOY SURVIVES SMALLPOX

1796

DOCTOR EDWARD JENNER has carried out a reckless experiment on a young boy.

He scratched some liquid from a smallpox blister into the arm of 12-year-old James Phipps. Smallpox is responsible for many deaths every year. How is it that the parents gave their consent? It seems to be a miracle that the boy has survived.

Doctor Jenner puts it down to "Scientific observation"! Apparently he has noticed that milkmaids never catch smallpox.

Although they often catch cowpox, a mild disease. He told our reporter, "I took some pus from a cowpox blister and scratched it into the arm of young James. He later developed cowpox, but soon recovered. Later I inoculated him with smallpox, but he did not show signs of the disease – I believe that he is now immune to it."

Where will all this experimenting end?

Will we all start growing horns as a result of the new cowpox inoculation?!!

a How is cowpox different from smallpox?
b How do you think cowpox is caught?
c What do you think gave Jenner the idea for inoculating against smallpox?
d Explain why you think James did not catch smallpox.
e Try to explain the reporter's attitude to Jenner's experiment.

Fighting off the enemy

1. Bacteria enter your body through a cut in your skin.

2. Your body makes antibodies to fight the invaders.

3. The bacteria are destroyed by the antibodies.

4. Antibodies stand by ready to fight off any future attack. The body is **immune**.

Do you remember from Book 8 how white blood cells defend your body? One sort 'eats' any germs it meets – let's call these 'killer cells'. The other sort makes **antibodies** – chemicals that stick the germs together and make them harmless. After any disease the antibodies stay in your blood for a while – this makes you immune.

▶ Study the cartoons. Use the information to write a brief explanation of what happens when harmful bacteria invade your body.

You can become immune by **vaccination**. A vaccine is a weak form of the disease microbe.

f Explain how you think vaccination works.
g Your body can make millions of ***different*** antibodies. Why do you think this is?

Mr Clean

Bob is the caretaker at the high school.
He's got a problem.
The label has come off his big bottle of disinfectant.
So he doesn't know how much to add to water before use.
If he adds too little, it won't kill the germs.
If he adds too much, it'll be expensive.
Help Bob out by finding the **smallest** amount of disinfectant that will kill the germs.

(Hint: You could use agar plates and paper discs with different concentrations of disinfectant on them.)

Your teacher will give you an agar plate with harmless bacteria growing on it.

How much disinfectant will you add?

How will you make it a **fair test**?

How long will you leave it to work?

How will you record your results?

Ask your teacher to check your plan, then try it out.

---

1 Copy and complete:
If you catch a disease and you don't get it again, you are . . . . to it.
Your body makes chemicals called . . . .
They stick the germs together and make them . . . .
The . . . . stay in your blood to give you immunity to the disease. A . . . . is a weak form of the disease microbe. It can be . . . . into your body or taken by mouth. It gives you . . . . to a disease.

2 Find out whether the following are true or false.
a) Tetanus is caused by germs getting into an open wound.
b) A pregnant woman cannot pass on rubella to her unborn child.
c) Smallpox vaccine is no longer given because the disease has been wiped out.
d) There is a low risk of whooping cough vaccine causing brain damage to some babies.

3 Why is it important that the following places are free from germs?
a) Swimming pools.
b) School kitchens.
c) Doctor's surgeries.

4 Try to find out what diseases people can be vaccinated against.
Which vaccines have you been given?

> **Things to do**

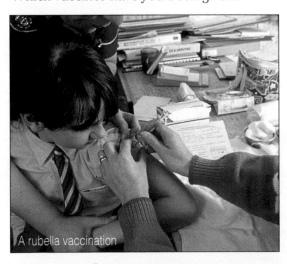
A rubella vaccination

The spread of disease

Look, this meat is full of maggots!

Yes, the meat has created the maggots.

Can you remember what microbes are?

400 years ago nobody had heard of microbes.

They didn't even know where other living things came from.

We now know that food rots because of microbes.
In the old days, most people thought rotting food **made** the microbes.

The mutton gravy has changed into new life.

BOILED

John Needham believed in this **spontaneous creation**. He thought that when an animal died parts of it formed new creatures.

Lazzaro Spallanzani showed that food does not go bad if the microbes are killed. He killed the microbes by sealing the food and then boiling it.

It's off!

In 1854 **Louis Pasteur** isolated microbes and added them to sterilised soup – they multiplied.

He was able to show that it was microbes that made wine and milk decay.

There is a vital **force** in all living things. When they die it produces microbes.

Felix Pouchet still believed in spontaneous creation. He came to opposite conclusions to Louis Pasteur.

I boiled the broth in each flask.

The microbes can't get into this flask. They get stuck in the neck.

BROTH BROTH

Pasteur's experiments were more reliable than Pouchet's. He proved that microbes caused diseases such as anthrax.

In the nineteenth century, hospitals were not very clean places. Microbes spread easily and wounds often became infected.

Women giving birth in hospitals sometimes died of fever afterwards. **Dr Ignaz Semmelweiss** noticed that doctors never washed their hands between patients.

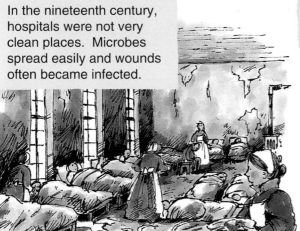

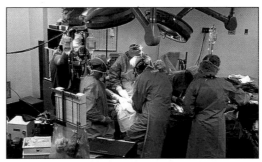

Our doctors are carrying the infection on their hands.

They must wash their hands in disinfectant between patients.

Disinfect

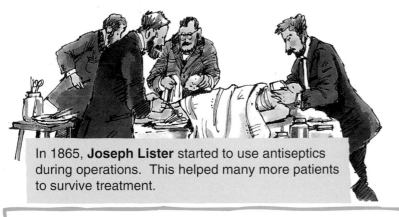

In 1865, **Joseph Lister** started to use antiseptics during operations. This helped many more patients to survive treatment.

Modern operating theatres are kept as free from microbes as possible.

1 Write down what you can remember about the 3 main types of microbes?

2 What happens if a bottle of milk is left open to the air?
Give your answer as if you agreed with John Needham and Felix Pouchet.

3 a) How was Louis Pasteur able to kill microbes in milk?
b) What do we call this process today?
c) Name 4 other ways in which microbes in food can be killed.

4 a) How did Semmelweiss discover that disease was spread in hospitals?
b) How was he able to reduce this spread of disease?

5 Look at the operating theatre in Lister's time.
a) What conditions can you see that reduce the spread of infection?
b) What things do not reduce this spread?
Now look at the modern-day operating theatre.
c) What precautions have been made in it to prevent the spread of infection?

Things to do

85

Questions

1 Ask your parents and grandparents some questions about their lifestyle.
   a) What sports and activities did they do when they were your age?
   b) Did they do them in school?
   c) How many sports and activities did they do outside school?
   d) What facilities did they have?
   e) How much time did they spend watching television or playing board games?
   What are your conclusions?
   Do you think they were fitter and more active than you are?

2 Suppose that you have a young kitten or puppy. Plan an investigation to measure its growth.
   How will you measure its growth (try 2 ways)?
   How often will you take measurements?
   How long do you think this investigation will take?
   How will you display your results?

3 Choose a topic, either alcohol abuse or solvent abuse.
   Make a leaflet about it, to go in a doctor's surgery.
   Write about the danger to health and how it can affect your body.
   If possible use drawings and photos from newspapers in your leaflet.

4 *Drug and solvent abuse costs the country millions of pounds every year.*
   Use the following headings to help you to explain this sentence: a) medical treatment   b) burglary and theft   c) catching the drug pushers.
   What actions do you think would reduce drug abuse?

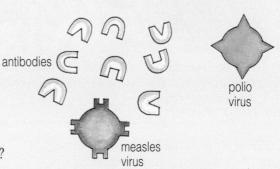

5 Look at the picture. It shows some of the antibodies that Martin has in his blood.
   a) Does Martin's blood contain antibodies to fight polio?
   b) Is he immune to polio?
   c) Can he catch polio?
   d) Does Martin have the antibodies in his blood to fight measles?
   e) Is he immune to measles?

6 Do some research and find out what operations were like in the 19th century.
   Draw a diagram or describe what you think the conditions were like.
   What are modern operating theatres like today?
   Draw a diagram or do some writing to show how conditions have improved.

7 Do you think that snooker is a sport?
   Write down any reasons that you can think of to support your answer.
   Now do the same for ice-skating, chess, and ballroom dancing.

Your life is full of forces.
Everything that you do needs a force – a push or a pull.

You use forces to move around, and to transfer energy.

In this topic, we'll look at forces as they move, as they turn, and as they exert a pressure.

Then we'll look at the force of gravity, and how it affects our Solar System.

Moving at speed

31a

a If you wanted to measure the speed of a bicycle, what 2 things would you have to measure?

b Write down the formula for calculating speed.

c A cyclist travels 50 m in 10 seconds. What is her average speed?

d Copy out this table and then complete it:

$$\text{average speed} = \frac{\textbf{distance travelled} \text{ (in metres)}}{\textbf{time taken} \text{ (in seconds)}}$$

	Distance travelled	Time taken	Average speed
an ant	20 cm	10 s	
a jogger		100 s	2 m/s
a car	100 m		20 m/s
a plane	2000 km	2 h	

e A cyclist can go at constant speed, or ***accelerate***, or ***decelerate***. Explain what these 2 bold words mean.

Balanced and unbalanced forces

If something is standing still, then a force is needed to start it moving. If it is already moving, then a force is needed to make it accelerate, or decelerate.
A force is also needed to make it change direction.

In the diagram, object **A** has a force on it, and so it will start to move and accelerate.

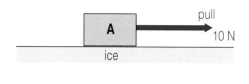

Object **B** has 2 forces on it:

The 2 forces are equal and opposite. They are **balanced**, so there is *no resultant force* and the object stays as it is.

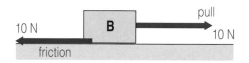

In diagram **C**, the 2 forces are not balanced:

f What is the resultant force on **C**?
Which way does the object move?

g Using a scale of 1 cm for 1 newton, draw an object with a force of 10 N pulling on it. Draw a friction force of 4 N. What is the resultant force?

Friction

▶ Look at the photo of the bicycle.

h Where on the bike is friction i) useful?
                                   ii) a nuisance?

i Explain how air resistance is used by a parachutist:

▶ Look at the photo of 2 car tyres:

j Which one is safer? Why do you think this is?

Safety matters

When a driver has to brake, it takes time for him to react. In that fraction of a second, the car can travel many metres. This is called the **thinking distance**.

You measured your reaction time earlier (page 53). For most people, when they are not expecting to brake, the reaction time is 0.7 second!

No seat belts! Testing cars with dummies

k Suppose you were driving at 20 m/s (this is 45 mph).
If your reaction time is 0.7 s, how far would you travel before you started to press the brake**?**

l How would this thinking distance be affected if the driver was tired**?**
What else could affect this thinking distance**?**

▶ The **braking distance** is the distance the car will travel **after** the brake is pressed.

m At 20 m/s (45 mph) on a dry road, with good brakes, the braking distance is 31 m.
What is the **total stopping distance?**

n On a wet road, the braking distance is **twice** as much. What is the total stopping distance then**?**

o What other things would affect the braking distance**?**

Shortest stopping distances, *on a dry road, with good brakes*

At 13 m/s *(30 mph)*

Thinking distance	Braking distance	Total stopping distance
9 m	14 m	23 m

At 22 m/s *(50 mph)*

Thinking distance	Braking distance	Total stopping distance
15 m	38 m	53 m

At 30 m/s *(70 mph)*

Thinking distance	Braking distance	Total stopping distance
21 m	75 m	96 m

The distances shown in car lengths are based on an average family car.

Finding your reaction time

- You can use the method of page 53 to find out how quickly you can react and reach a brake pedal with your foot:

- Find your reaction time when you are thinking of something else. For example, talking to someone.

- Imagine you are travelling at 20 m/s (45 mph) on a wet road. Use your reaction time to calculate the total stopping distance.

1 Copy and complete:
a) The formula for speed is:
b) The units for speed are m/s (. . . . per . . . .) or km/h (. . . . per . . . .) or m.p.h. (. . . . per . . . .).
c) When the forces on an object are equal and opposite, we say they are . . . .
d) If the forces are balanced, there is no . . . . force.

2 A girl jogs at 2 m/s.
a) How far would she go in 10 seconds?
b) How long would she take to go 400 m?

3 Copy and complete this table:

Name of runner	Distance (metres)	Time taken (seconds)	Speed (m/s)
Ayesha	60	10	
Ben		5	8
Chris	100		5
Donna	400		4

4 Suppose a driver can see only 25 m because it is misty. What should his maximum speed be?

Things to do

Just a moment

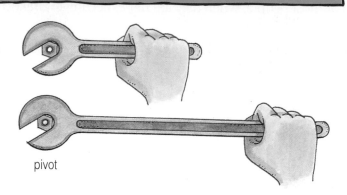

▶ The diagram shows 2 spanners:
Which spanner would you use to turn a very tight nut?
How can you make it even easier to turn the nut?

▶ Which is the best place to push on a door to open it –
at the hinge or at the door edge?

▶ Some water-taps are hard for old people or invalids to
turn. Design a better tap for an old person.

pivot

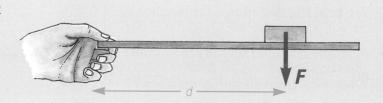

Hold a ruler at the very end, and put an object on it
(for example, a rubber):

● Put the object at different positions on the ruler.
What do you notice?

● Try a heavier object, at different distances.

d   **F**

The turning effect depends on 2 things:
● the size of the force,
● the distance of the force from the pivot.

The turning effect of a force is called its **moment**.
The moment is calculated by:

Moment of the force =	**force**	×	**distance from pivot**
	(in newtons)		(in metres)

Moments are measured in units called **newton-metre (N m)**.

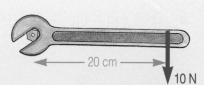

Example 1
A car-driver is tightening a nut.

She exerts a 10 N force, 20 cm
from the nut:

How big is the turning effect?

— 20 cm —
10 N

Answer
Distance from pivot = 20 cm = 0.2 m

Moment = force × distance from pivot

= 10 N × 0.2 m

= <u>2 N m</u>

a If the driver applies a force of 100 N,
40 cm from the pivot, what is the moment?

b A boy pushes a door with a force of 10 N,
60 cm from the hinge. What is the moment?

Moments in balance

Here is a see-saw:

The big girl has a moment which is turning in a clockwise direction.

c Which way is the small boy's moment turning?

d Why do you think that the small boy can balance the big girl?

When the see-saw is balanced, and not moving, it is 'in equilibrium'.

Then: ⟮ the **anti-clockwise moments** = the **clockwise moments** ⟯

This is called **the principle of moments** (or **the law of levers**).

Testing the principle of moments

Your teacher can give you a Help Sheet for this.

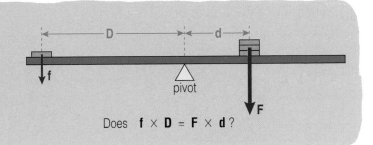

- You can use a ruler as a see-saw, and add weights:

- Work out the clockwise and anti-clockwise moments. What do you find?

Does **f** × **D** = **F** × **d** ?

Example 2

A pole-vaulter is holding his pole:

His left hand acts as a pivot.
You can assume that the weight of the pole (50 N) acts at the centre of the pole, 1 m from the pivot.
How hard must his right hand push down?

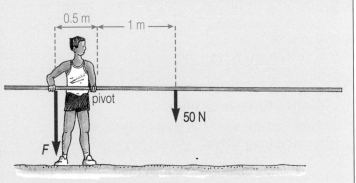

Answer

When balanced ('in equilibrium'):

anti-clockwise moments = clockwise moments

$$F \times 0.5 = 50 \times 1$$

$$F = \frac{50}{0.5} = \underline{100 \text{ newtons}}$$

---

1 Copy and complete:
a) The turning effect (or . . . .) of a force is equal to the force multiplied by the . . . . from the . . . . Its unit is . . . .
b) The principle of moments states that, when an object is balanced and not moving, the anti-clockwise . . . . are . . . . to the . . . . moments.

2 Explain why it is difficult to steer a bike by gripping the centre of the handle-bars.

3 The diagrams show metre rules balanced at their centres.
What is the weight of a) *X*? and b) *Y*?

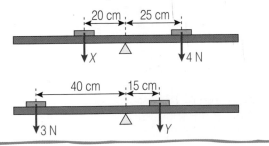

Levers

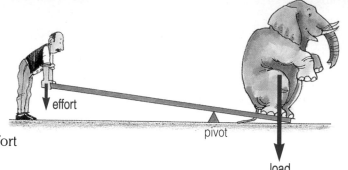

In the last lesson you started to look at levers.
A lever is a simple **machine**. It helps us to
do work more easily.
Here is a lever being used to lift a big **load**:

The lever can turn about a pivot (or 'fulcrum').
The man is applying an **effort** force.

a Where would you move the pivot to make the effort
even smaller?

b Which moves through a bigger distance – the man's
hands or the elephant?

Example

A wheelbarrow with its load weighs
300 newtons.

The weight acts at a distance of 0.5 m
from the centre of the wheel (the pivot).

What force is needed to lift the handles,
which are 1.5 m from the centre of the
wheel?

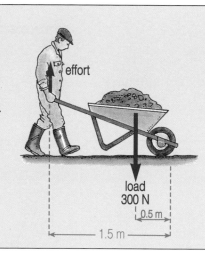

Answer

Use the principle of moments (p. 89).

When balanced ('in equilibrium'):

$$\left(\begin{array}{c}\text{clockwise}\\ \text{moment}\end{array} = \begin{array}{c}\text{anti-clockwise}\\ \text{moment}\end{array}\right)$$

$$\text{effort} \times 1.5 = 300 \times 0.5$$

$$\text{effort} = \underline{100 \text{ newtons}}$$

- Design a wheelbarrow that
would need even less effort.

This lever is a **force-magnifier**.

c Where is there a lever in your body used as a
distance-magnifier? (*Hint:* see page 50.)

Here are some common machines using levers.
For each one you should be able to find the **pivot**, and
decide the positions of the **effort** force and the **load** force.
Your teacher will give you
a Help Sheet for this.

fishing
rod

claw
hammer

pliers

bottle
opener

A balancing act

The gymnast is balanced on a beam:

Each part of her body is pulled down by gravity.

All the clockwise moments of the left-hand parts of her body are **balanced** by the anti-clockwise moments of the right-hand parts.

It's just as though all her weight is one force acting at one point **G**.
G is called the **centre of gravity**.

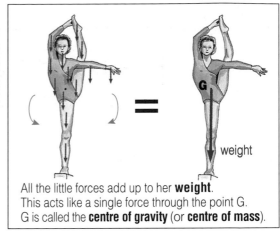

All the little forces add up to her **weight**.
This acts like a single force through the point G.
G is called the **centre of gravity** (or **centre of mass**).

d What would happen if her centre of gravity was not directly over her foot**?**

e Where is the centre of gravity of a metre rule**?**

Stability

If something is **stable**, it does not topple over.
Use a box or match-box to investigate what makes an object stable.

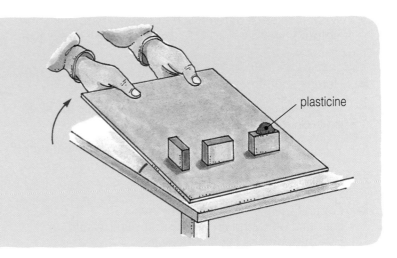

plasticine

- You can use plasticine to raise or lower the centre of gravity.

- To make the box more stable, should it have
  i)   a high or a low centre of gravity**?**
  ii) a narrow or a wide base**?**

f Which is more stable: a racing-car or a double-decker bus**?**

g How are these 3 objects made stable**?**

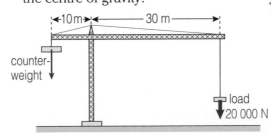

Things to do

1 Copy and complete:
a) A lever can be a . . . .-magnifier or a . . . .-magnifier.
b) The centre of . . . . (centre of mass) is the point through which the whole . . . . of the object seems to act.
c) A stable object should have a . . . . centre of . . . . , and a . . . . base.

2 Which is more stable: a milk-bottle
a) full? or b) $\frac{1}{4}$-full of milk?
Draw diagrams of the bottles on a slope to explain your answer.

3 The diagram shows a tall crane with a counter-weight to balance the load.
a) Calculate the size of the counter-weight.
b) What can you say about the position of the centre of gravity?

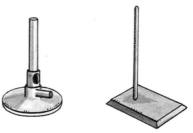

counter-weight

load
20 000 N

Under pressure

▶ You can push a drawing-pin into the table:

But you can't push your thumb into the table, even though you use a bigger force.

Why do you think this is**?**

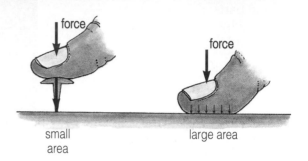

force

force

small area

large area

▶ The pin-point has a small area. All the force is concentrated in that area, to give a high **pressure**.

With your thumb, the same force is spread out over a larger area. The pressure is smaller.

a What is the real difference between a sharp knife and a blunt knife**?**

▶ Here is another example:

Why does the boy sink into the snow, while the skier stays on top**?**

What are snow-shoes? Why do eskimoes wear them**?**

▶ Look at the pictures shown below.
For each one, explain what is happening, and why.
Use these words in your answers:

high/low **pressure**   **force**   small/large **area**

1 This bag is always hurting me.

2 No problem, but my heels keep getting stuck.

Which is best for a muddy garden?

3

4 This chair is always leaving marks on the carpet.

Can you solve this problem for me?

To calculate the pressure you need to know 2 things:
• the force exerted (in newtons)
• the area it is spread over (in cm² or m²).

If the area is in cm², then the unit of pressure is newtons per square centimetre (**N/cm²**).

If the area is in m², then the unit of pressure is newtons per square metre (**N/m²**).
This unit is also called a **pascal (Pa)**. 1 Pa = 1 N/m².

In fact:

$$\text{Pressure} = \frac{\textbf{force} \ \text{(in newtons)}}{\textbf{area} \ \text{(in cm}^2 \text{ or m}^2)}$$

Example

Nellie the elephant weighs 40 000 newtons.

She stands on one foot, of area 1000 cm².

What is the pressure on the ground?

Answer

$$\text{Pressure} = \frac{\text{force}}{\text{area}}$$

$$= \frac{40\ 000\ \text{N}}{1000\ \text{cm}^2}$$

$$= \underline{40\ \text{N/cm}^2}$$

40 000 N

b Use the same method to calculate the pressure when a woman weighing 500 N stands on a stiletto heel of area 1 cm².

500 N

c Now compare these two pressures.
Which exerts the bigger pressure – the elephant or the shoe?
Which exerts the bigger force?

Shoe pressure

Plan a way to work out the pressure that you exert on the ground.

- Which 2 things do you have to measure?
- How can you do this?

- If you have time, do the investigation.

- Who makes the biggest and least pressures in your class?

---

1 Copy and complete:
a) The formula for pressure is:
b) Its units are . . . . per square centimetre (N/cm²) or . . . . per square metre (N/m², also called . . . .).

2 Explain the following:
a) It hurts to hold a heavy parcel by the string.
b) It is more comfortable to sit on a bed than on a fence.
c) Heavy lorries may have 8 rear wheels.

3 Design a beach-chair suitable for use on soft sand. Sketch your design.

4 What is the pressure when a force of 12 N pushes on an area of 2 square metres?

5 A man weighs 800 N. The total area of his 2 shoes is 400 cm².
a) What is the pressure on the ground?
b) He puts on some snow-shoes of total area 1600 cm². What is the pressure now?

6 This box weighs 100 N.
a) Calculate the area of each face.
b) Calculate the pressures when i) the red, ii) the yellow, and iii) the blue faces are on the ground.

5 cm   10 cm   2 cm

Things to do

Pressure all around

Pressure in liquids

▶ Why do you think deep-sea divers have to wear special clothes?
Why do submarines have to be strong?

Yes – it is because of the **pressure** on them.

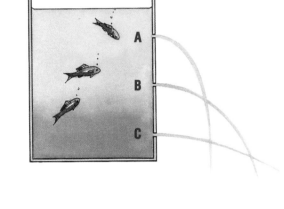

▶ Water is surprisingly heavy. A tank of goldfish
probably weighs more than you do!

The weight of water presses down and exerts a pressure.
As a fish swims deeper, the pressure on it increases
more and more.

This tank has 3 holes in the side:

You can see that the water is spurting out under pressure.

Which jet of water is spurting out farthest?

Where is the pressure greatest – at A, B, or C?

▶ Here is a side-view of a lake made by a dam:

The length of each arrow shows the size of the pressure.

a Where is the pressure least?

b Where is the pressure greatest?

c Why does the dam need to be thicker at
the bottom than at the top?

d Which forces are holding up the boat?
These forces are called the **upthrust**.

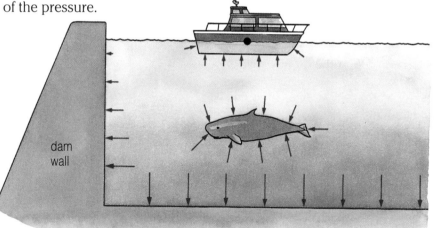

dam
wall

e The weight of the boat is 1000 N.
Where does this force act?

f The upthrust and the weight of the boat
are **balanced** forces. What does this mean?

g How big is the upthrust in this case?

▶ The pressure of a liquid can be used to
work **hydraulic** machines:

What happens if you push in piston A?

Where is this used on a car?

syringe

water

A

B

Pressure of air

Just as fish live at the bottom of a sea of water, we are living at the bottom of a 'sea' of air.
This air is called the **atmosphere**.

It exerts a pressure on us (just as the sea squeezes a fish).
This is called **atmospheric pressure**.

▶ If you blow up a balloon, you blow millions of tiny air **molecules** into it:

  These molecules bounce around inside the balloon. Whenever a molecule hits the balloon, it gives the rubber a tiny push. Millions of these tiny pushes add up, to make the air pressure.

  You are being punched on the nose billions of times each second by these tiny air molecules!

Can it be crushed?

Your teacher will show you an experiment with a metal can:

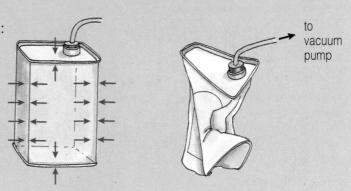

to vacuum pump

- At the start, the can has air inside and outside. The air molecules are bouncing on the inside and the outside.

- If a pump is used to take the air out of the can, what happens?

- Can you explain this? Try to use these words:
    molecules   air pressure

Sucking a straw

When you 'suck' on a straw, you use your lungs to lower the pressure inside the straw.

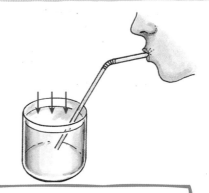

Explain why the liquid moves up, using these words:
    molecules   air pressure

---

1 Copy and complete:
a) The pressure in a liquid is .... at the bottom than at the top.
b) A boat floats because the water pressure makes an .... force on it.
c) Air pressure is caused by billions of tiny .... bouncing around.

2 What happens to the air pressure as you go up a mountain? Why is this?

3 Explain why:
a) You can fill a bucket from a downstairs tap faster than from an upstairs tap.
b) Aeroplanes are often 'pressurised'.
c) Astronauts wear space-suits.

4 Alex says, "A vacuum cleaner works rather like a drinking straw."
Explain what you think he means, using the words: molecule, pressure.

Things to do

Ideas about gravity

350 B.C. **Aristotle** thought that heavy objects contained a substance called gravity.

He thought that light objects had a substance called levity.

> I think heavy objects fall faster than light objects.

> That's an interesting idea. Have you checked it with an experiment?

> No need. I just know it must be true.

For 2000 years, people believed this!

Then, in 1589, **Galileo** shocked people by actually doing experiments!

He is supposed to have used the leaning tower at Pisa:

> Gasp!

> Look! The heavy weight and the light weight both land together.

They both have exactly the same acceleration.

> But why does a feather fall more slowly?

> Ah! — that's because of air resistance.

> If there was no air it would fall like an apple.

In 1666, **Isaac Newton** was thinking about gravity:

> The apple moves because it is pulled to the Earth by a force.

> I wonder if the Moon is also pulled to the Earth by gravity.

> Is that why the Moon travels in orbit round the Earth?

Isaac calculated how much the Earth pulled on the Moon.
He found that the farther the distance, the weaker the force of gravity.
At twice the distance, the force is $\frac{1}{4}$.
At 3 times the distance, the force is $\frac{1}{9}$.

ewton took his
eas further . . .

If the Earth pulls on the Moon, then the Moon must pull on the Earth.

And the Sun must pull on the Earth

and on all the other planets.

Sir Isaac Newton
1642–1727

So the Solar System is held together by the force of GRAVITY!

Isaac worked out a formula:

This means that _every_ object attracts _every_ other object.

$$\text{Force} = G \times \frac{\text{mass 1} \times \text{mass 2}}{\text{distance squared}}$$

He published his ideas in a famous book.

Principia Mathematica ~ 1686 ~

The force between 2 bottles on a shelf is only $\frac{1}{200\ 000\ 000}$ of a newton

– but the pull of the Earth on you is about 500 N – your **weight**.

Newton's ideas seemed to work perfectly, until . . .

1916 **Albert Einstein** thought about the effect of gravity on space itself.

Let's think of space as like a rubber sheet.

A big mass like the Sun will 'warp' or bend the space near it.

Like this marble a space-ship will travel in a curve. BUT — so also will a ray of light.

So, light is affected by gravity. (An experiment proved it later.)

If the gravity of a star is very, very strong, it will pull so hard that the light from the star cannot escape . . . . . . it is a **black hole**!

---

1 Use the idea of gravity to explain:
a) Why is an astronaut lighter on the Moon than on the Earth?
b) What evidence is there that Saturn exerts a gravitational pull?
c) Which object has the greatest pull in our Solar System?
d) Why do the planets not travel in straight lines?

2 The diagram shows 4 cups on the Earth's surface. Copy the diagram and draw each cup half-filled with water. Which way is 'up'?

3 An astronaut on the Moon dropped a feather and a hammer at the same time. They hit the ground together. Why does this happen on the Moon but not on Earth?

Things to do

Rockets and satellites

Anna throws a ball horizontally:
The ball moves in a curve.

a   Why does the ball not move in a straight line**?**

b   What happens if she throws it harder**?**

c   What happens if she fires a bullet horizontally**?**

Escaping from the Earth

Imagine firing a gun from the top of a very high mountain:

The bullet will fall back to Earth, just like a ball. It is pulled by gravity. This is shown at **A** in the diagram.

What if the bullet could be fired faster**?** It would go farther, but still fall to Earth. Look at **B** and **C**.

Suppose the bullet could be fired even faster, at 25 times the speed of sound. It would still fall towards Earth but, because the Earth is curved, it would stay the same height above the ground. Look at **D**.

It is now in orbit. It is a **satellite**.

d   What can happen if it travels even faster than **D?**
Draw a diagram of this.

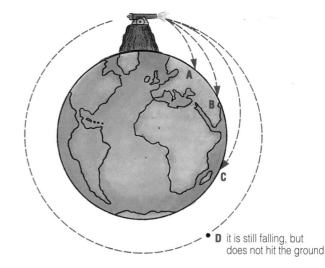

D it is still falling, but does not hit the ground

You can't do this with a gun, but you can with a **rocket**.
It needs a speed of about 29 000 km per hour (18 000 mph).

A satellite moves very fast, but it can seem to be standing still !
If the satellite is put at just the right height and speed, it takes **24 hours** to go round the Earth once.
This is the same time as the Earth takes to spin round once – so the satellite appears to stay over one place !
This is called a **geo-stationary** satellite.

Rockets

- Blow up a balloon and then let go.
  What happens**?** Why**?**

  As the air rushes backwards, the balloon moves forwards. A rocket works in the same way.

- Your teacher may show you a water rocket, ⚠ using compressed air.
  What happens when the water is forced out**?** Why**?**

The space-shuttle taking off.

A communications satellite.

Using satellites

Communications satellites can be used to send telephone messages or TV pictures:

We use a geo-stationary satellite. It moves with the Earth, and stays over Europe all the time.

You can use a 'dish' aerial on your house to get the signal.

e Why are the dishes used in the north of Scotland bigger than those used in the south of England?

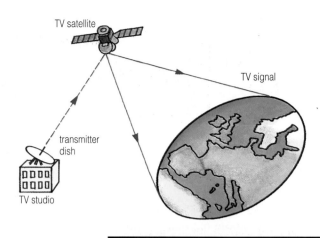

Weather satellites are useful. They take photos of the weather, and send the pictures back to Earth by radio.

f Look at the weather picture shown below. Write down all the conclusions you can draw from it.

Land survey satellites are very useful. These are lower satellites that take photos in great detail. They can warn of forest fires and water pollution; show healthy and diseased crops; and help us to find oil.

Military satellites are used for spying.

Navigation satellites are used by ships and planes. Pilots can find where they are, anywhere on Earth, to within 10 metres !

Astronomy satellites carry telescopes. They can take very sharp pictures of planets, because they are outside the Earth's atmosphere.

The Earth seen from a satellite

A weather picture of the UK/Europe. What conclusions can you draw?

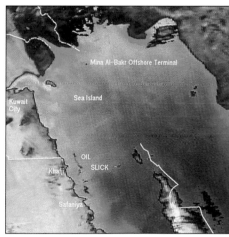

An oil slick polluting the sea. Which part of the world is this?

This is London. Can you see the bridges over the river Thames?

---

1 Copy and complete:
a) All objects are pulled to the Earth by . . . .
b) If it travels fast enough, a satellite can stay in . . . . even though it is falling towards Earth all the time.

2 Why do satellites not need to be streamlined?

3 The diagram shows a firework rocket: As it flies through the air, there are 3 forces on it. Copy the diagram.
a) Which 3 arrows show the 3 forces?
b) Label the 3 arrows, using these words: **weight** **air resistance** **thrust**
c) What can you say about these forces when the rocket is just taking off?
d) Why does the rocket come back down?

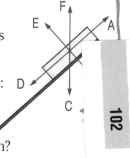

The Solar System

The Sun is a star, like all the other stars in the sky.

a Why does the Sun look brighter than the other stars?

b How many hours does it take for the Earth to spin round once?
c Explain why we have day-time and night-time.

d The Sun 'rises' in the East. Which way are we travelling, now?
e At night, all the stars appear to move slowly to the West. Why?

The Sun – our nearest star. On the same scale, the Earth is about the size of this full stop .

The diagram shows the Earth on its journey round the Sun:

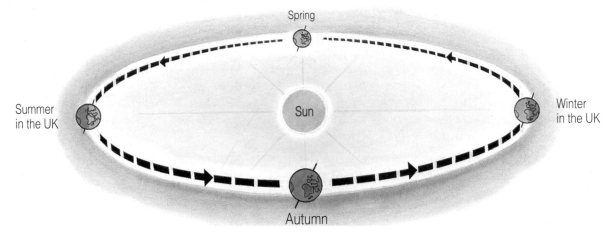

f How long does it take for the Earth to make one complete journey round the Sun?
g How many times does the Earth spin on its axis while it makes this journey?
h The Earth travels in an ellipse. Why does it not travel in a straight line?

The Earth's axis is always **_tilted_** at $23\frac{1}{2}°$, like this:

In summer, our part of the Earth is tilted towards the Sun.
You can see this in the diagram above.
This means that the Sun appears higher in the sky to us.

i Why is it warmer in summer?
j Why is winter colder?

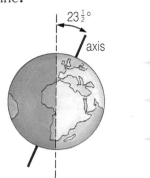

k The Moon is in orbit round the Earth. How long does it take for 1 orbit?
l Why does the Moon shine? What happens if it goes into the Earth's shadow?

Use a lamp and a ball to 'model' the Sun and the Earth.
Use your model to show: 1) day and night,
2) a year,
3) summer and winter.

The planets

The diagram shows the planets orbiting our Sun (not to scale):

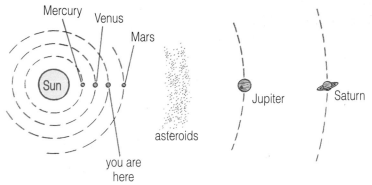

m Pluto is not shown on the diagram. Where would it be?

n How many planets are there? Write down their names in order. Then find a way to memorise them.

o Which 2 planets are nearest to Earth? Which of these is hotter than Earth?

p Which 2 are the biggest planets? Which of these has rings round it?

q Which planet do you think is the coldest? Why is this?

r Which planet goes round the Sun in the shortest time?

s The planets travel in curved orbits. What is the name of the force that pulls them from a straight line?

t Planets and stars both look like bright dots in the sky. What difference is there in the way they send light to us?

u Planets are smaller than stars, but they often look as bright as stars. What conclusion can you draw from this?

Jupiter

The photo shows Voyager-2.
This is a space-probe or 'artificial satellite'.
It has been used to explore the Solar System.

v Why has it not been used to explore outside the Solar System?

w Why has it not carried people?

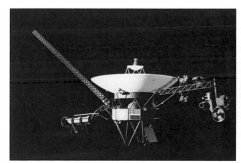

The Voyager-2 space-probe travelled at 20 000 mph. After 4 years it passed Saturn.

---

1 Copy and complete:
a) The . . . . is the centre of the . . . . System.
b) The names of the 9 planets (in order) are:
c) The coldest planet is . . . . This is because it is the farthest from the . . . .
d) The planets do not travel in . . . . lines. Their orbits are . . . . This is because of the gravitational . . . . of the . . . ., pulling on each planet.
e) The . . . . shine only by reflected . . . ., like the Moon.

2 Here is a list of objects:
star planet universe moon galaxy
a) Put them in order of size (smallest first).
b) For each one, write a sentence to explain what it is.

3 Why do you think Pluto was the last planet to be discovered?

4 Explain why you think life developed on Earth and not on other planets.

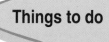

Things to do

Questions

1 The graph shows how far a cyclist travels in 10 seconds:

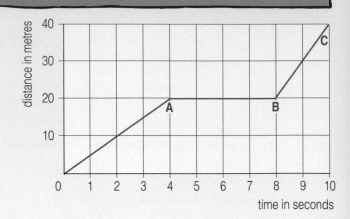

Use the graph to answer these questions.
   a) How far does she go in the first 4 seconds?
   b) What was her speed during the first 4 seconds?
   c) What was her speed between 4 and 8 seconds?
   d) What was her average speed for the whole journey?
   e) During which part of her journey was she travelling fastest?

2 The diagram shows an aeroplane. It has 4 forces on it:

The names of the 4 forces are
   ● the **lift** from the wings,
   ● the **weight** of the plane,
   ● the **drag** of the air resistance,
   ● the **thrust** of the engine.

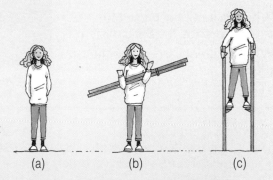

   a) Sketch the plane and put the correct label against each force.
   b) If the lift is greater than the weight, what happens to the plane?
   c) If the thrust is greater than the drag, what happens?

3 The diagram shows a metre rule balanced on a pivot:

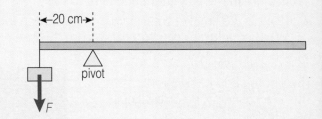

The weight of the rule is 1 N.
   a) Where does the weight of the rule act?
   b) Re-draw the diagram, showing the weight of the rule.
   c) How far is this force from the pivot?
   d) What is the value of F?
   e) What is the total force down on the pivot?
   f) What is the force exerted by the pivot on the rule?

4 Jackie has a pair of stilts:

She weighs 400 N and the stilts weigh 100 N.
Each of her shoes has an area of 150 cm².
The bottom of each stilt has an area of 25 cm².
Calculate the pressure on the ground in each of the diagrams:

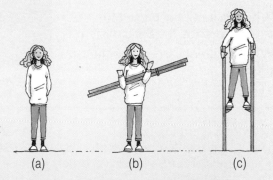

5 A car with 4 wheels has the tyres at a pressure of 20 N/cm².
Each tyre has an area of 100 cm² in contact with the road.
   a) What is the weight of the car?
   b) If 1 kg weighs 10 N, what is the mass of the car (in kg)?

6 Paul says, "When you look at the stars, you are looking back in time." What does he mean?

Matter

32

Everything around us is a solid, a liquid or a gas.
We ourselves are made of solid, liquid and gas.
These are the 3 states of matter.
But what do the states have in common?
How are they different?

In this topic you'll find out.

32a Solid, liquid or gas?

When did you last go to a fair?

▶ Look at the picture:

a Can you name:
  i) 2 solids,
  ii) 2 liquids,
  iii) 2 gases? (Clue: you might not be able to see the gases!)

Solid, liquid and gas are the **3 states of matter**.

Which state?

Your teacher will give you some substances.
Decide whether each one is a solid, a liquid or a gas.
Look carefully at the substances. Think back to your work in
Spotlight Science 7.
Copy and complete the table. Use ✓ for yes and ✗ for no.
A few answers have been done for you.

Yes, It's a liquid!

Property	Solid	Liquid	Gas
Is it runny?		✓	
Is it hard?			
Is it heavy?			
Can it be poured?	✗		
Does it have a fixed shape?			
Does it have a fixed volume?			
Is it easily squashed?			✓
Is it easily stirred?	✗		✓
Is it dense? (Heavy for its volume)			

This bottle of cola contains gas:

b Where is the gas?

c What is the gas called?

d What happens when you open a can of fizzy drink . . .

. . . straight from the fridge?   or    . . . just off the shelf?

Is there any difference?

Getting rid of the fizz

Quarter fill a test-tube with cold fizzy water.
Add a few drops of universal indicator.
What do you see?
The carbon dioxide dissolved in the water makes it a weak acid.

Warm the tube **gently** shaking a little all the time.
Let the fizzy water boil slowly.
Look at the colour of the universal indicator.
What do you see?
Try to explain what is happening.

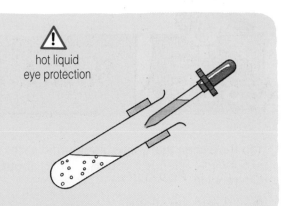

! hot liquid
eye protection

Time the fizz

In this investigation you'll be working with a solid, a liquid and a gas.
Stomach powder is the solid. It is added to the liquid, water, and a gas is made.

Your task is to use this reaction to measure time.
Your device must measure 40 seconds exactly.
Plan how you can do this.
Your teacher will give you some stomach powder.
Show your teacher your plan. Ask for the other apparatus you need.
Each group can have a stop-clock for the tests.
The stop-clock will be taken away when your device is tested!

Which group is the most accurate?

Well, you said you wanted a watch for your birthday!

---

1 Copy and complete:
a) Solids have a . . . . shape.
b) Liquids and . . . . take the shape of the container.
c) Gases are . . . . dense than solids and liquids.
d) Solids and liquids are . . . . to squash.
e) . . . . and . . . . can be poured.
f) Solids and liquids have a . . . . volume.

2 Which properties of solids, liquids and gases are important for these sports?
a) rock climbing
b) water skiing
c) hot-air ballooning
d) hockey
e) ice-skating

3 Classify each of these as solid, liquid or gas at room temperature.

| paper | ice | mud | glass | smoke |
| air | wax | carbon dioxide | petrol |

Are any hard to classify? Why?
Write about your ideas.

4 Sam filled a syringe with water. He held the end against a rubber stopper. He pushed the plunger.

He then did the test with air in the syringe.
Then he did the test with pieces of wood in the syringe. Describe what he would have noticed in each of the 3 tests.

Things to do

What's the matter?

You have seen that solids, liquids and gases behave in different ways.
In *Spotlight Science 7* you used ideas about **particles** to explain the
differences.

▶ Look at the photos.
How does each one suggest that matter is made of particles?

a Blue water?

b Hot curry?

c Sweet mug?

d Lovely smell?

Particle tests

Now try these simple tests. For each one, write down what you notice.
What does each one tell you about particles? Write down your ideas.
Think about differences between solids, liquids and gases.

Purple shades

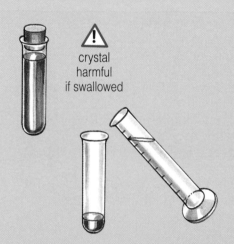

crystal
harmful
if swallowed

1. Take one large purple crystal. Put it in a test-tube.
   Add 10 cm³ water. Cork the tube. Carefully shake it to
   dissolve the crystal.

2. Take 1 cm³ of this solution in another test-tube.
   Add 9 cm³ water. Cork the tube. Carefully shake it.

3. Repeat step 2 again and again. Do this until you can't see the
   pink colour any more.

How many times did you repeat step 2?
What does this tell you about the particles in the crystal?

Lost in spaces?

Measure 25 cm³ sand in a measuring cylinder.
Measure 25 cm³ dried peas in another cylinder.
Predict the total volume when the 2 solids are added together
and mixed.

Now mix the 2 solids. Shake the substances well. Let the
mixture settle.
What is the ***total*** volume?

Warm air
Gently warm the tube of air for one minute. What do you see?
As soon as you stop heating, lift the delivery tube out of the water.

suck-back

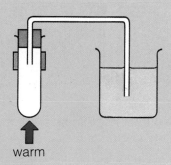

warm

'Dry ice'

'Dry ice' is solid carbon dioxide.
The solid turns easily to gas. It is stored in pressurised containers.

A *small* volume of solid gives a *large* volume of gas.
Does this tell you anything about particles in solids and gases?

Have you seen dry ice being used at pop concerts?

Rising balloons

A balloon rises if it is less dense than the air around it.

How does the air in a hot-air balloon become less dense than the air outside?
Try to explain your idea by drawing particles.

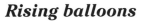

heat → ?

cold air   hot air

1 Copy and complete.
Choose the correct word from the 2 in brackets.
a) All matter is made of . . . . (particles/solids)
b) The particles are very . . . . (small/large)
c) In a gas, the particles are . . . . (more/less) spread out than in a liquid.

2 Soluble aspirin tablets are used to treat headaches.

What happens to the particles in the tablet when it is dropped in water?
Draw pictures to help you to explain.
Use ○ for a water particle.
Use ● for an aspirin particle.

3 This coffee filter collects the coffee grains. Why does the water pass through the filter paper?

4 To make a balloon lighter than air you could fill it with a light gas.
Hydrogen is a light gas.
a) Why isn't hydrogen used to fill passenger balloons?
b) Find out all you can about the Hindenburg.

Things to do

Particles on the move

▶ Draw 3 diagrams to show how you think particles are arranged in a solid, a liquid and a gas.

How do your diagrams explain that:

a solids are hard to compress (squash)?

b liquids can be poured?

c gases are the shape of their container?

In Book 7 you learnt that materials **expand** when they get hot. They **contract** when they cool down.

d What does *expand* mean?

e What does *contract* mean?

f When a solid expands, what do you think happens to the particles?

▶ Look at your answers to **d**, **e** and **f**.
Use these to help you with the photo questions.

g Why is mercury used in thermometers?

i Boiling water should not be poured into a cold glass. Why not?

h Railway tracks contain small gaps. Why do they have these?

Watching for movement

Do particles move? Try some of these tests to find out.

A blue move?
Before you do this test, predict what will happen.

Put a few blue crystals in the bottom of a beaker.
Carefully pour water on the top.
Do not shake or stir.
Leave the beaker for a few days.
Draw pictures to show what happens.

Do you think particles move?
Write down or draw what you think happens to the particles.

Smoke signals?
Your teacher will show you this experiment.

When fumes from the acid and ammonia meet, white smoke forms.

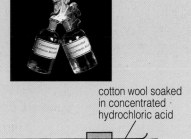

What do you think will happen in this experiment?
Predict **exactly** what you will see.

Your teacher will do this experiment.
Try to explain what you see.

cotton wool soaked in concentrated ammonia solution

cotton wool soaked in concentrated hydrochloric acid

cork

A brown move?
Your teacher will show you the bromine experiment.

What happens when a gas jar of air is put on top of a gas jar of bromine?
Do you think the particles move?
Write down or draw what you think happens to the particles.

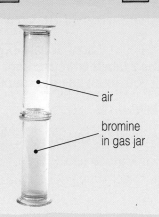

air

bromine in gas jar

Diffusion

Liquid and gas particles can move and mix. They do this without being stirred or shaken. This is called **diffusion**.

Have you ever smelt freshly baked bread?
Particles of gas are released from the bread. They **diffuse** through the air. You can smell the bread throughout the room.

1 Copy and complete:

a) These are the particles in a . . . .

b) These are the particles in a . . . .

c) These are the particles in a . . . .

2 Robert Brown was a Scottish scientist. He studied pollen grains in water. Find out about what he saw. This is called Brownian motion.

3 Helium is a lighter gas than air. Gas particles can diffuse through balloon rubber. This is why balloons go down.

Which balloon do you think will go down first? Why?

Things to do

Gases and pressure

▶ Copy out each label. Say whether it is for a **solid**, a **liquid** or a **gas**. (Clue: there are 2 labels for each!)

The particles are very close together.

The particles are far apart. They move in all directions.

The particles are quite close together.

The particles move about quickly.

The particles do not move about. They vibrate.

The particles move about.

▶ Look at the 2 labels you have chosen for gases. These tell you about **gas pressure**.

Gas pressure . . .

. . . keeps a balloon blown up.

. . . tells us about the weather.

. . . gives us a comfy bike ride!

Gas pressure

What causes the pressure? Particles help us to understand.
Think about gas inside a balloon.
The particles move around very quickly.
They move in all directions. Some particles hit each other.
Others hit the wall of the balloon. Those that hit the wall give a force on each unit of area of the balloon. This is called the **pressure** of the gas. (Look at page 94 to remind yourself about pressure.)

Think about gases

Make some predictions. Discuss these in your group.

1 Think of a gas in a closed box. What happens if you heat the gas? Do you think the pressure will increase or decrease? Try to explain using the idea of particles.

2 Think of a gas in a syringe. The plunger can move in and out. What happens to the plunger if you heat the gas? Try to explain using the idea of particles.

Check your predictions with your teacher.

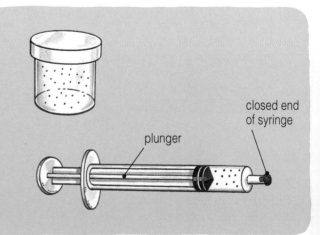

closed end of syringe

plunger

Moving gases

Your teacher will show you an experiment.
Try to explain what you see.
Use your ideas about gas pressure and diffusion.

Your teacher will put some natural gas into the beaker.

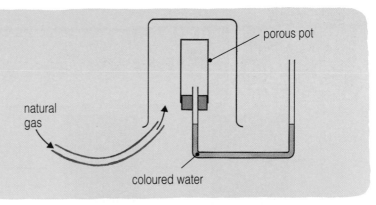

natural gas

porous pot

coloured water

Liquid gases

Gases can be turned into liquids. One way to do this is to put the gas in a pressurised container. We say the gas is **compressed** or stored **under pressure**.

You may have seen some tankers like this on the road:
Liquid nitrogen is very useful. It is very cold.

Lots of foods are frozen by spraying them with liquid nitrogen.

a Why does **compressing** a gas turn it to liquid? Use particles to explain.

b Why do we freeze food?

c Are frozen foods good for you? Write about your ideas.

Propane and butane can also be stored as liquids.

d What are these gases used for?

e What are the dangers of these gases?

---

1 Copy and complete:
Particles in a gas . . . . quickly in . . . . directions. When they hit the . . . . of a container this is called the gas . . . . This is the . . . . on each unit of area. Gas particles move more . . . . when they are heated. As the gas is heated in the container, the pressure . . . .

2

Why shouldn't you put this near to heat?

3 Why are gases stored and transported as liquids?

4 Look at these boiling points of gases that are in the air.

xenon	−108°C	krypton	−153°C
argon	−186°C	nitrogen	−196°C
oxygen	−183°C	helium	−269°C
	neon	−246°C	

To collect the gases, air is cooled so it becomes liquid. The liquid air is slowly warmed so the gases boil off.
a) Which 2 gases have the closest boiling points?
b) When liquid air is warmed, which boils off first – oxygen, argon or nitrogen?
c) Which gas is the most common in the air?
d) Which gas is needed for burning?

Things to do

Energy for a change

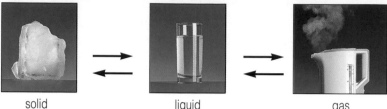

solid   liquid   gas

Water is usually found as a liquid. But water can be a solid (ice) or a gas (steam).
Ice, water and steam are the same chemical substance (H_2O).
When water turns into ice or steam we say it is **changing state**.

▶ Sketch the pictures of the 3 states of water. Write a label next
to each arrow. Choose the correct label from this list:

     boil (or evaporate)   **melt**   **freeze**   **condense**

a   At what temperature does water boil?

b   At what temperatures does ice melt?

Liquids into solids

How do you turn a solid into a liquid? How do you turn a liquid into a solid?
In this experiment you will make a solid melt by heating it. Then you
will let the liquid cool slowly. What do you think will happen?

- Put a few spatula measures of the solid in a test-tube.
- Clamp the tube in a warm water bath.
- Heat up the water bath until the solid melts.
- When the temperature of the liquid reaches 75°C,
  switch off your Bunsen.
  Leave the substance to cool in the water bath.
- Record the temperature of the substance every minute as it cools.
- Stir carefully.
- Take readings every minute until the temperature
  reaches 50°C.
- Leave the apparatus to cool.

hot
eye protection

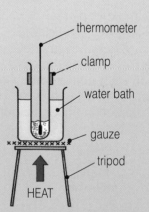

thermometer

clamp

water bath

gauze

tripod

HEAT

Plot a graph of your results.
Try to explain the shape of your graph.

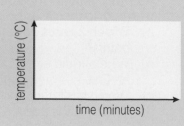

temperature (°C)

time (minutes)

Feeling cool?

Dip your finger into water.
Dip the same finger of the other hand into alcohol.
Hold your fingers out in front of you.

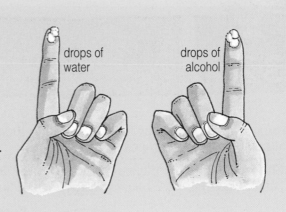

drops of water   drops of alcohol

c   Which liquid cools your skin most?

d   Which liquid evaporates faster?

e   Try to explain these results using the idea of moving particles.

thermometer

beaker

ice

Hassan studied some ice melting.
He stirred crushed ice in a beaker.
He took the temperature of the ice every 2 minutes.
These are his results:

Time (minutes)	0	2	4	6	8	10	12	14	16	18	20
Temperature (°C)	-4	-2	0	0	0	0	0	0	0	2	5

f   At what temperature did the ice melt?

g   Ice melts when it is heated. Where did the heat come from in this experiment?

h   Why didn't the temperature rise between 4 and 16 minutes? (Clue: think about particles!)

Salt lowers the freezing point of water.

i   Why do we put salt on icy roads in winter?

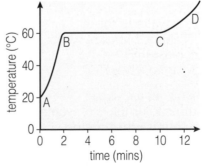

Things to do

1   Copy and complete using **heat** or **cool**:
a) To turn a solid to a liquid you need to . . . . it.
b) To turn a liquid to a gas you need to . . . . it.
c) To turn a gas to a liquid you need to . . . . it.
d) To turn a liquid to a solid you need to . . . . it.

2   Use the words from the box to describe
a) melting point   b) boiling point.

solid	liquid	gas	temperature

3   You looked at the water cycle in Book 8. Use the words below to help explain the cycle.

evaporate	sea	Sun	cloud
	rain	condense	

Draw a simple picture of the cycle.

4   Look at this heating curve for a solid substance X:

a) What is the state of X from:
i) A to B?   ii) B to C?   iii) C to D?
b) What is the melting point of X?
c) X is being heated. Why does the temperature stay steady between B and C?
d) What do you think happens if heating carries on after 12 minutes?

Wet or dry?

Do you think it's a good day for drying clothes today?
What makes a good drying day?

a Choose the best conditions. Write out your choices. Why did you choose these? Explain why these conditions are best.

 a wet day

a windy day

a cool day

a hot day

a still day

a dry day

b Do clothes dry better spread out or squashed up? Why?

c Where do you think the water goes when it leaves the washing?

When clothes dry, the water **changes state**. It turns from *liquid* to *gas* (vapour). This change of state is a useful one for us. But some changes of state can cause problems . . . .

Cooling the air

Put 3 ice cubes and about 6 spatula measures of salt into a beaker. This makes a very cold mixture.

Watch the outside of the beaker closely.
Write down everything you see.

Condensation

Even though you can't see it, there is water in the air.
The air in a warm kitchen contains about 2 litres of water. But the air can only hold a certain amount of water.

Do you remember the water cycle?
Warm air can hold more water than cold air.
If air is cooled, the water vapour turns to droplets of water. We call this **condensation**. The water vapour is **condensing**.

Condensing is the reverse of **evaporating**.

GAS (VAPOUR) 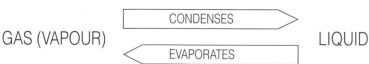 LIQUID

Is condensation a problem where you live? What do you think causes it?

► Look at the inside of Sundial Cottage.
In your group make a list of all the things causing condensation.

Soak it up

Some chemicals absorb water. They soak it up.
They can be used to reduce condensation problems.
Your teacher will give you some chemicals.

Plan an investigation to see which is best at absorbing water.

Ask your teacher to check your plan. Then do the investigation.

Products like these can reduce condensation problems.

1 Copy and complete:
a) Condensing is the reverse of . . . .
b) Condense means to turn gas (vapour) to . . . .
c) Evaporate means to turn . . . . to gas (vapour).

2 Why do people put anti-freeze in cars? How does it work?

3 Tumble-dryers are useful.
They dry clothes on a wet day.
a) What happens inside a tumble-dryer?
b) Explain how these conditions help to dry clothes.
c) Write about a disadvantage of using a tumble-dryer.

4 a) How can you reduce condensation without spending lots of money?
Make a leaflet for householders to give them some tips.
b) If you can afford them, there are other ways to reduce condensation.
Collect information about these.
(D.I.Y. stores may be helpful.)

Things to do

Dissolving

Do you like drinking tea?
There's a lot of science in action when you make tea.

▶ Look at what you do:

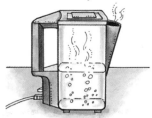

Boiling the water.

Brewing the tea.

Adding milk and sugar.

Write about the particles in each step shown above.
Where are they? What is happening to them?
Start with the water particles in the kettle. Finish with the particles
in your cup of milky sweet tea.
Try to use some or all of these words and phrases:

moving slowly	*moving more quickly*	*steam*	*diffuse*	*soluble*
insoluble	*close together*	*far apart*	*dissolve*	*mix*

Sugar dissolves in a hot cup of tea. It dissolves in the water. It
makes a **solution**. Sugar is **soluble**.
In a solution the substance which dissolves is the **solute**. Sugar is
the **solute**. The water dissolves the sugar. The water is the
solvent.

solute   +   solvent   ⟶   solution

In most solutions the solvent is water. But other substances can be
solvents.

Have you ever had any clothes dry-cleaned?
Dry-cleaning uses solvents without water in them. These are called
non-aqueous solvents.

a   What type of stains can dry-cleaning remove?

b   Why don't we dry-clean **all** our clothes?

Nail varnish remover is another non-aqueous solvent.

c   What is its chemical name**?**

Clean nails

Paint some nail varnish on a glass slide.
Leave it to dry for a few minutes.
Test the 3 solvents your teacher will give you.
Which is best at removing the varnish**?**

Some solutes are very soluble in a solvent but they may be
insoluble in another solvent.
They have different **solubilities** in different solvents.

A stain remover

Plan an investigation on solvents.
Which solvent is best at removing stains**?**

⚠ Some solvents are very flammable.
Make sure there are no Bunsens
alight in the lab.

Your teacher will give you some substances which stain.
Examples could be:

ball-point pen	felt-tip pen	grease
paint grass	coffee	tea
orange juice	tomato sauce	

Ask your teacher to check your plan. Then do the investigation.

Dissolving quickly

Think about all the things that affect dissolving.
How could you get a sugar cube to dissolve as quickly as possible**?**

▶   Make a list of your ideas.

Things to do

1   Copy and complete:
a)   A substance which . . . . is soluble.
b)   A substance which does not . . . . is
   insoluble.
c)   solute + solvent → . . . .
d)   Solvents without . . . . are non-aqueous.
e)   Solutes have different . . . . in different
   solvents.

2   Which of these are soluble in water?
a)   sand
b)   salt
c)   chalk
d)   butter
e)   wax
f)   sugar

3   Sea-water is a solution. Name
a solute and the solvent in sea-water.

4   What's the difference between these felt-
tip pens?

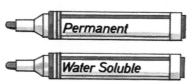

5   Does the mass of a substance change
when it dissolves?
Make a prediction. Say why you think this
to be true.
Then plan an investigation to test your
prediction.

Questions

Speech bubbles: "What's the matter?" "I'm in a state" "I'm in three"

1 Name some things in your body which are
a) solid b) liquid c) gas.

2 Sam adds a spoonful of sugar to his tea.
Why doesn't the full cup overflow?
Draw particle diagrams to explain.

3
Fizzo **is the fizziest orange drink you can buy.
It leaves the others flat.**

Plan an investigation to see which drink contains the most fizz.

4 Sue's teacher drew some particle diagrams for her class. But the labels got muddled.
Copy out the diagrams. Choose the right label to write under each diagram.

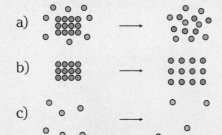

a)

b)

c)

Labels
a solid expanding
a gas expanding
a sugar cube dissolving in water

5 Iodine is a solid which turns straight to a gas when heated.
It doesn't form a liquid.
Draw particle diagrams to show the change from solid to gas.

6 Tracy says "Balloons go down faster in hot weather than in cold weather." Do you agree with her idea?
Plan an investigation to test this. (The investigation must be done on one day!)

thermometer

water out

7 Are new substances made when things melt?
Explain your answer.

8 Evaporation and condensation are happening here:
a) What is this process called?
b) Explain how the process works to get pure water.

water in

HEAT

Variation

33

We inherit many of our features from our parents.
They are passed on from one generation to the next.

In this topic you are going to find out how things are inherited.

In this topic:
- **33a** *The same but different*
- **33b** *A design for life*
- **33c** *From generation to generation*
- **33d** *Pick and mix*

The same but different

Look at the kittens in the picture:
They are all from the same litter.

a In what ways do you think they look alike**?**

b In what ways do you think they look different**?**

▶ Look around at the people in your class.
   They have a lot in common: they are all human for a start!
   But they also have features that are different.
   Make a list of some of these differences.

Why do we look like we do?

We get some of our features from our parents. We **inherit** them.
Other features do not come from our parents.
These features are caused by the way we lead our life.
We call these features **environmental**.

Can you roll your tongue like the girl in the photograph**?**

You can't learn how to do it. You have either inherited it from your
parents or you haven't.

The soccer player in the photograph has a lot of natural ability.
Do you think that this is inherited or environmental**?**
But to be a top-class player, strength, agility and stamina are needed.
Do you think that these are inherited or environmental**?**

▶ Copy out the following list of features.
   Write (i) after those that you think are inherited,
   and   (e) after those that you think are environmental.

shape of nose	neat writing	freckles	hair colour
hair length	scars	skill at languages	an accent
eye colour	good at sport	blood group	size of feet

How do you measure up?

Nobody's the same, we are all unique!
Collect the following information about yourself and others in your class:

> eye colour   height   left-handed *or* right-handed   shoe size
>
> length of index finger   hair colour   tongue rolling   ear lobes

Record your findings.
Some things vary **gradually**.

c Draw a bar-chart to show the number of people in your class with different length index fingers. What do you find?

Other things are more **clear-cut**. For instance there are only a few different types of eye colour.

d Draw a bar-chart to show the number of people in your class with different colour eyes. What do you find?

▶ Look at the graph of the height of some pupils:

e How many children are less than 160 cm?

f What is the most common height?

g Do you think that the variation shown on the graph is gradual or clear-cut?

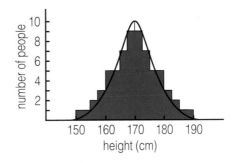

▶ Look at the graph of the hair colour of some pupils:

h What is the most common hair colour in the class?

i How is this graph different from the graph for height?

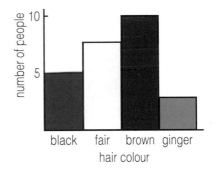

---

1 Copy and complete:
We . . . . many features from our parents.
Other things, like being able to ride a bike, we . . . . during our lifetime. We say that they are due to the . . . .
Some variation, like height, is . . . . Other variation, such as eye colour, is . . . .

2 Libby has just come home from 2 weeks in Majorca.
Do you think her sun-tan is inherited?
Explain your answer.

3 Mike says "I think red hair and being good at sport are both inherited."
Do you agree or disagree? Give your reasons.

4 Look at the picture of a litter of puppies:
a) What features have the puppies inherited from their mother?
b) What features have the puppies inherited from their father?

Things to do

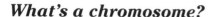

A design for life

Have you ever heard someone say of a new baby, "Isn't she like her father?" or "Doesn't he have his mother's eyes?"

What things do you think you have inherited from your parents?

What's a chromosome?

How do we inherit things from our parents?

The **instructions** for designing a new baby are found in 2 places:

- the egg cell of the mother, and
- the sperm cell of the father.

a Which part of these cells do you think contains these instructions?

Most cells in your body contain a nucleus.
Each nucleus contains **chromosomes**.
It is the chromosomes that carry the instructions.

▶ Look at the photo:

b What do the chromosomes look like?

c Are they all the same size and shape?

d How many are there?

In most human cells there are 46 chromosomes.
We can put them into 23 pairs that are identical.

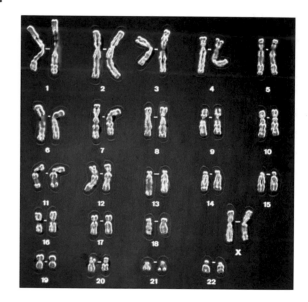

Halving and doubling

When a sperm cell or an egg cell is made, the chromosomes in each pair split up.

e So how many chromosomes will there be in the sperm or egg now?
Do you remember what happens when a sperm fertilises an egg?

▶ Look at the diagram:

f How many chromosomes does a fertilised egg contain?

g Where have these chromosomes come from?

h What do you think would happen at fertilisation if the sperm and the egg each contained 46 chromosomes?

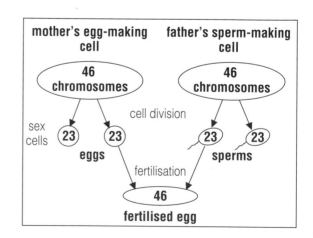

mother's egg-making cell | father's sperm-making cell

46 chromosomes | 46 chromosomes

cell division

sex cells | 23 | 23 | 23 | 23

eggs | sperms

fertilisation

46

fertilised egg

Looking at chromosomes

Scientists can make slides of human chromosomes.
Your teacher will give you a sheet showing what these
chromosomes look like.

- Count the number of chromosomes.
- Cut out your chromosomes and count them again to make sure
  you haven't lost any.
- Arrange them on a sheet of paper. Start with the largest and end
  with the smallest.
- Arrange your chromosomes in pairs according to size and
  pattern of banding.
- Stick down your chromosomes neatly in their pairs.

i   Are these chromosomes from a female or a male?

j   How do you know?

k   What do you think the bands on each chromosome might be?

Genes

Genes contain the instructions that we inherit.
Genes control certain features like eye colour.

▶ Look at the diagram:

l   How many genes do you think there are for each feature?

m Where are they found?

n What do you notice about the position of genes on a pair of
chromosomes?
Each band on a chromosome represents one gene.

Key to genes
- ● eye colour
- × hair colour
- ▲ tongue rolling
- ■ height
- ● nose length
- ✳ skin colour
- ■ making haemoglobin
- ∨ build of body

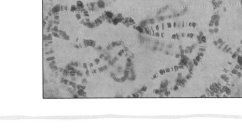

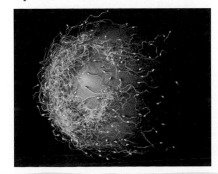

Things to do

1 Copy and complete:
Inside the nucleus of each cell there are
thread-like shapes, called . . . .
These are made up of . . . .
These . . . . contain instructions to control
how the . . . . works.
They also contain information which is . . . .
from one generation to the next.

2 How many chromosomes are there in a
human sperm or a human egg?
How many are there in other human cells?
Why do you think these numbers are
different?

3 Where are genes found?
What do genes do?
Genes are made of the chemical called DNA.
Try to find out what DNA stands for.

From generation to generation

They keep gerbils in Billy's school.
He spends a lot of time feeding and looking after them.
Last year a brown male mated with a white female.
Billy was disappointed when there were no white baby gerbils in the litter. They all had brown fur.

a What do you think controls the fur colour in gerbils?

b How many genes are there for fur colour?

The gene for fur colour is found on a chromosome.
You know that chromosomes occur in identical **pairs**.
So there must be a **pair** of genes for each feature.
Here is a diagram to explain what happened with Billy's gerbils:

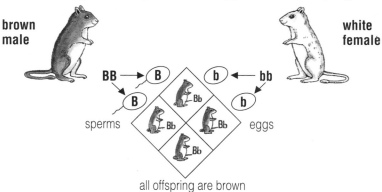

all offspring are brown

c How many brown genes (B) are needed to give a brown gerbil?

d How many white genes (b) are needed to give a white gerbil?

The brown gene gives a 'stronger' message than the white gene.
We say that it is **dominant**.
We call the 'weaker' white gene **recessive**.

What do you think would happen if one of the brown gerbils (Bb) was mated with another brown gerbil (Bb)?

▶ Copy and complete this diagram to find out:

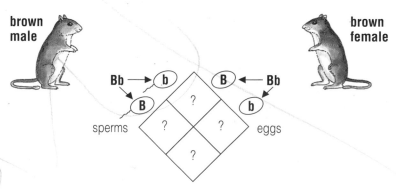

e How many brown gerbils would you expect there to be?

f How many white gerbils would you expect there to be?

The red-eyed fly!

The fruit fly can have red or white eyes.
Red eye (R) is dominant to white eye (r).

Your teacher will give you 50 red beads to represent the red eye genes (R)
and 50 white beads to represent the white eye genes (r).

- Take 2 plastic cups.
- Into each cup put 25 red beads and 25 white beads.
- Stir the beads up well.

g One cup represents a female fly and the other represents a male fly.
What colour eyes would each one have?

- Now place 3 empty cups side-by-side in front of you.
- Close your eyes and take a bead from each cup.
  Look at them.
  If they are both red, put them in your left-hand cup.
  If they are both white, put them in your right-hand cup.
  If one is red and one is white, put them in the middle cup.
- Carry on until you have used up all your beads.
- Count the number of pairs of beads in each cup.
  Write them down in a table like this:

	Red	Red and white	White
number of pairs			

h From your results, how many flies would have red eyes and how many would have white?
(Change this to a ratio if you can.)

i Why were you asked to take **one** bead from each cup?

j Why were you asked to close your eyes when taking the beads?

Things to do

1 Copy and complete:
For every feature there are . . . . genes. Some genes give a 'stronger' message than others and are called . . . . Genes giving a 'weaker' message are called . . . .
In each sperm and each . . . . there is only . . . . gene for each feature. When the . . . . fertilises the egg, ... genes will be present for each feature.

2 If Billy was to breed only white gerbils, why do you think their babies would always be white? Why do you think that brown gerbils don't always produce brown baby gerbils?

3 A red tulip was crossed (fertilised) with a white tulip. The seeds produced only red tulips.
a) Which colour is dominant?
b) These red tulips were then self-fertilised. How many red to white tulips would you expect?

4 Why do you think that a white gerbil would find it hard to survive in the wild? Why do you still get white gerbils in litters?

Pick and mix

Vicki's dad keeps racing pigeons.
She helps to look after them.
They are related to wild pigeons, but have been specially bred.
They have to fly long distances but always return home.

a   What features do you think have been bred into racing pigeons?

Selective breeding means that we breed in the features that we want and breed out the features that we don't want.

▶   Write down a list of animals and plants that humans have selectively bred.
     Why do you think humans have selectively bred these animals and plants?

Calypso fruit

A new type of fruit has been discovered on a tropical island.
It has an amazing taste, but only when it is just ripe.
The skin is covered with hairs and it is difficult to remove.
It has a bright orange colour that often attracts birds.
The number of its seeds varies and they are very bitter.
It is said to be very good for the digestion since it contains a lot of fibre.
The calypso fruits are hard to pick because the stem has lots of thorns.

b   Draw a diagram of what you think the calypso fruit looks like.

c   What features would you try to breed out?

d   What features would you keep?

e   What would your calypso fruit look like after selective breeding?

This little piggy . . .

Our modern pig is descended from the wild pig.

▶   Look at the photos:

Bacon pig

Wild pig

f   Which features do you think have been bred into the modern pig?

g   Which features do you think have been bred out of it?

h   Do you think the modern pig could survive in the wild?
       Give your reasons.

Supercow!

Farmers can now breed better cattle.
New breeds of cattle produce more milk and more beef.

Artificial insemination means that sperm can be taken from the best bulls and put directly into the best cows.
This means that the farmer no longer has to keep bulls of his own.

i Why do you think this is an advantage to the farmer?

Eggs from the best cows can be removed and fertilised with bull sperm in a test-tube.
The fertilised egg is then put back into the mother cow.
These are called **embryo transplants**.

j What do you think are the advantages to breeders of:
  i) artificial insemination?
  ii) embryo transplants?

k Why do you think is it important to keep alive some of the old-fashioned breeds of cattle?

In your groups, discuss whether you think that artificial insemination and embryo transplants should be used on farm animals.

---

1 Make a list of 5 animals or plants that you think have been 'improved' by selective breeding. For each one, say how you think this is useful to humans.

2 A lot of cereals originally came from the Middle East.
What features do you think have been bred into varieties that are grown in Britain?

3 What features do you think have been bred into these dogs:
a) pekingese?   b) sheep dog?
c) bloodhound?

4 Humans have selectively bred modern varieties of wheat from wild wheat.
These have greater yield, improved disease resistance and ripen over a shorter time.
How do you think these 3 features have helped the farmer?

Things to do

Questions

1 What features do you think that you have inherited from
a) your mother?   b) your father?
If you have a sister or brother, have they inherited the same features?

2 Bob and Baz are identical twins:
What features have they inherited from their parents?
What features are the result of their environment?

3 Some pupils did a survey on the size of foxglove fruits.
Here are their results:

Length of fruit (mm)	20	21	22	23	24	25	26	27	28	29
Number collected	4	6	14	22	30	26	18	12	12	3

a) Draw a bar-chart of their results.
b) What sort of variation do you think this shows?

4 When a tall plant was crossed with a short plant, all the seeds produced tall plants.
a) Which size of plant do you think was recessive?
b) These tall plants were then self-fertilised.
How many tall plants and how many short plants would you expect to get?

5 Breeding racehorses is a million-pound industry.
What sort of features do you think would be bred into a champion racehorse?

6 If animals of 2 different species mate they produce a **hybrid**.
The tigon in the picture resulted when a tiger and a lion mated in captivity.
a) What do you think were the parents of a leopon and a zeedonk?
b) Invent your own animal from 2 different species and draw it.
c) Hybrids are usually sterile (they cannot produce offspring).
Why do you think that the survival of some species would be threatened if they bred with other species in the wild?

tigon

7 Look at the table of 2 breeds of sheep:

Feature	Welsh Mountain breed	Border Leicester breed
adult mass (kg)	30–32	73–77
number of lambs born per female (ewe)	1	2
temperament	wild	docile
fleece per ewe (kg)	1	3
growth rate	slow	fast

a) What features do you think have been bred into the Border Leicester?
b) How do these make it a successful sheep?
c) Hill farmers often cross Welsh Mountain ewes with Border Leicester rams. Why do you think this is?

Chemical reactions 34

Chemical reactions keep you alive.
Today you'll probably be eating food made by chemical reactions.
Reactions may also be keeping you warm.

Some reactions are so powerful they can put a rocket into space . . . .

What a change!

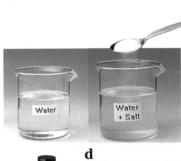

What can you remember about **chemical changes?**

a Write down 3 things that might happen in a chemical change.

Scientists talk about 2 kinds of changes –
chemical changes and **physical changes**.
In a **chemical change** a new substance is made.
It's not easy to get the substance you started with back again.
We say the change is **irreversible**.
In a **physical change** no new substance is made.
We say the change is **reversible**.

▶ Look at the photos of some changes.
For each one, say if you think it is a chemical change, or a physical change. Explain why.

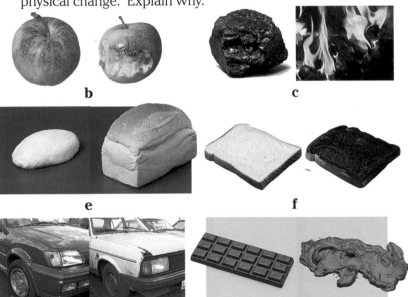

b   c   d

e   f   g

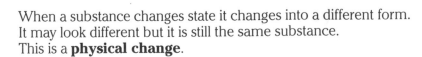

h   i   j

When a new substance is made, a chemical reaction must happen.
This is a **chemical change**.
The new substance is called a **product**.
You have seen lots of chemical reactions already.
Do you remember burning magnesium?

magnesium + oxygen ⟶ magnesium oxide

▶ Copy and complete these word equations for reactions:

copper + ... ⟶ copper oxide

iron   + ... ⟶ iron chloride

When a substance changes state it changes into a different form.
It may look different but it is still the same substance.
This is a **physical change**.

132

Does the mass change?

Do you think **mass** changes ... during a physical change?
... during a chemical change?
Predict what your conclusions will be before you do each test.

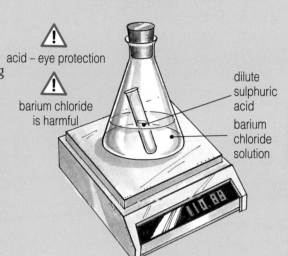

beaker

melting ice

49.68

Test 1 – A physical change
- Put a cube of ice in a beaker.
- Quickly put the beaker on the top-pan balance. Measure its mass.
- Leave the beaker until the cube has half melted. Measure its mass again.
- When the ice has all melted, measure its mass again.

What do you notice about the mass?

Test 2 – A chemical change
- Half fill a small tube with dilute sulphuric acid. Carefully put it inside a small conical flask.
- Measure out 25 cm^3 of barium chloride solution in a measuring cylinder.
- Carefully use a teat pipette to transfer the solution into the flask.
  Do not drop any solution into the test-tube.
- Put a stopper on the flask. ***Do not let any acid spill into the solution***. Measure the mass of the apparatus.
- Now tip the flask very gently so the 2 liquids mix. How do you know there is a reaction? Measure the mass of the apparatus again.

What do you notice about the mass?

⚠ acid – eye protection

⚠ barium chloride is harmful

dilute sulphuric acid

barium chloride solution

110.88

In a **physical change**, the mass stays the same. This is because no new substance is made. The substance just changes its form.

In a **chemical change**, the *total* mass stays the same. This is because the new substances must be made from the substances already there. The chemical elements are just combining together in different ways.

---

1 Copy and complete:
a) In a .... change, a new substance is made.
b) In a .... change, no new substance is made.
c) In a chemical change, the total mass ....
d) In a physical change, the mass ....

2 Melting is a physical change.
a) Describe what happens to the particles as a solid melts.
b) Use your answer to a) to explain why the mass stays the same in a physical change.

3 Which of these are chemical changes?
a) Making soap from vegetable oil.
b) Boiling some water.
c) Burning natural gas.
d) Making aluminium cans from aluminium metal.
e) Making coffee by adding water to coffee powder.
f) Making glass from sand.

Things to do

Palmolive

Making salts

The word *salt* probably makes you think of something you put on your chips!
But in science a **salt** is much more than this.

In this lesson you can make lots of *different* salts.
To do this you will start with an **acid**.

a Write down everything you know about acids. Include these words if you can.

pH	alkali	strong	red	weak	neutral

An acid can be changed into a salt – by a **chemical reaction**.

Acids and metals

Acids react with **metals** to make **salts**.

acid – eye protection

Making zinc sulphate

Add zinc powder to dilute sulphuric acid and stir.

When no more zinc dissolves, filter the mixture.

Carefully evaporate the filtrate to half its original volume.
Then leave it to cool.

eye protection

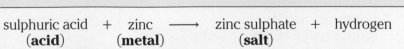

sulphuric acid	+	zinc	$\longrightarrow$	zinc sulphate	+	hydrogen
(acid)		**(metal)**		**(salt)**		

b Look at the photos. Which one shows the hydrogen being made**?**

c Why should you keep adding zinc until *no more dissolves***?**

d What do you see when you evaporate and then cool the solution**?**

e What is the name of the solid made**?** This is the product.

If you try this experiment, use the Help Sheet.

Acids and bases

Acids react with **bases** to make **salts**. The base **neutralises** the acid.

| acid + base ⟶ salt + water |

Bases are the oxides, hydroxides or carbonates of metals. All these are bases.

Making copper sulphate

acid – eye protection

Add copper oxide to warm dilute sulphuric acid and stir.

When no more copper oxide dissolves, filter the mixture.

Carefully evaporate the filtrate to half its original volume. Then leave it to cool.

eye protection

| sulphuric acid + copper oxide ⟶ copper sulphate + water |
| **(acid)** **(base)** **(salt)** |

f How can you tell there is a chemical reaction here?

g Which substance is left in the filter paper?

h What is the name of the solid made? This is the product.

If the base is copper carbonate you can still make copper sulphate the same way. (You don't have to warm the acid though.)

| sulphuric acid + copper carbonate ⟶ copper sulphate + water + carbon dioxide |

i What causes the fizzing in this reaction?

If you try these experiments, use the Help Sheets.

Salts made from **sulphuric acid** are **sulphates**.
Salts made from **hydrochloric acid** are **chlorides**.
Salts made from **nitric acid** are **nitrates**.

---

1 Copy and complete:
a) Acids react with metals to make .... and ....
b) Acids react with bases to make .... and ....
c) acid + ... ⟶ salt + ...
d) Bases are the oxides, ... or .... of metals.
e) Bases neutralise ....
f) Sulphates are made from .... acid.
g) Chlorides are made from .... acid.
h) Nitrates are made from .... acid.

2 To make copper sulphate you have to react copper *oxide* with sulphuric acid. Why can't you just use copper with acid? (Clue: think about the Reactivity Series.)

3 Some solutions were tested with pH paper:

solution	A	B	C	D	E
pH value	9	1	5	13	7

a) Say whether each solution is acidic, alkaline or neutral.
b) What colour does the pH paper turn with i) D? ii) E? iii) B?
c) Which solution is the most acidic?
d) Which solution could be pure water?

4 Acid rain causes problems. Think about the reactions of acids.
a) What happens when acid rain falls on metal?
b) Limestone is calcium carbonate. What happens when acid rain falls on limestone rock?

Things to do

Salt of the Earth

▶ Look at these bags of fertilisers:
The 3 main chemical elements in fertilisers are:
- nitrogen (N),
- phosphorus (P),
- potassium (K).

The elements are in compounds in the fertiliser.

a Which of these fertilisers:
  i) contain nitrogen?
  ii) contain phosphorus?
  iii) contain all 3 elements?

b What do fertilisers do? Why do we use them?
(Hint: look at Topic 24 in Book 8 if you need help.)

Rupa and Tim are talking about fertilisers.

I think it's best to put the fertiliser in the soil before you plant the seeds.

No. You should plant the seeds first and then add the fertiliser.

Who do you think is right?
Plan an investigation to find out.
In the next activity you can make a fertiliser.
You can use it to carry out your investigation.

Making a fertiliser

You can make a simple fertiliser called ammonium sulphate in the lab.

Ammonium sulphate has the formula $(NH_4)_2SO_4$.
c Which chemical elements does it contain?

Ammonium sulphate is a salt. It is made by neutralising an acid. In *Spotlight Science 7* you learnt that **alkalis** neutralise acids. An alkali is a special kind of base – it dissolves in water.

The reaction to make a fertiliser is a neutralisation.

$$\text{acid} + \text{alkali} \longrightarrow \text{salt} + \text{water}$$
$$\quad\;\;\text{(base)}$$

Sodium hydroxide is a base.
It is also an alkali.

Copper oxide is a base. It is
not an alkali.

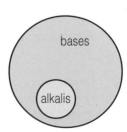

bases

alkalis

Making ammonium sulphate

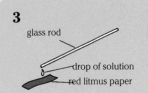

⚠ acid – eye protection

1
dilute sulphuric acid
conical flask

Put 20 cm³ of dilute sulphuric acid into a conical flask.

2
stand
ammonia solution
burette
glass rod
dilute sulphuric acid

Fill a burette with ammonia solution. Add 2 cm³ of ammonia solution to the acid.
Stir the mixture with a glass rod.

3
glass rod
drop of solution
red litmus paper

Take a drop of solution on the glass rod and wipe it on a piece of red litmus paper.

4

Does the paper turn blue? If not, repeat steps 2 and 3. Do this until the red litmus turns blue.

The litmus turns blue when enough alkali has been added.
The acid has been neutralised.

sulphuric acid + **ammonia solution** ⟶ **ammonium sulphate** + **water**
(acid) (alkali) (salt)

5
ammonium sulphate solution
gauze
hot
HEAT

⚠ Pour the solution into an evaporating basin.
Carefully evaporate the solution by heating it gently.
Evaporate until only half of the original solution is left.

6

Leave the basin to cool. Crystals of ammonium sulphate will form slowly.
Filter the crystals from any solution left.
Dry them between filter papers.

What does your fertiliser look like?
You can use this fertiliser to carry out your investigation (page 136).

---

1 Copy and complete:
a) 3 common elements in fertilisers are . . . . , ... and . . . .
b) NP fertilisers contain . . . . and . . . .
c) An . . . . is a base which dissolves in water.
d) Ammonium sulphate is made from dilute . . . . acid.

2 On packets of fertiliser you often see numbers. These are NPK ratios. They tell you how much nitrogen, phosphorus and potassium the fertiliser contains.
16.8.24 means 16%N 8%P 24%K.

0.24.24	15.15.21	25.0.16	27.5.5
1	**2**	**3**	**4**

a) Which fertiliser contains most nitrogen?
b) Which fertiliser contains least nitrogen?
c) Which one is NK fertiliser?
d) Which fertiliser contains the same % of nitrogen as phosphorus?

3 Visit a garden centre. Look at packets of fertilisers recommended for growing
i) fruit (e.g. tomatoes)
ii) grass
iii) flowers
a) Make a list of NPK values for these fertilisers.
b) Can you draw any conclusions about the elements needed to grow certain crops?

4 What are *organic vegetables*?
Why do some people want to buy these even if they are more expensive?

Things to do

34d Useful reactions

Some reactions are useful. Others, like rusting, are not useful.

▶ What is a **useful** reaction?
What do you think makes a reaction useful?
Write down your ideas.

Most chemical reactions are useful.

Neutralisation

acid + base ⟶ salt + water

This is a **neutralisation**.
You know that this reaction can be useful. Fertiliser can be made this way.
But other acid + base reactions are useful too:

This base helps to neutralise stomach acid.

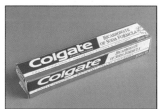

Acid in your mouth can dissolve tooth enamel.
Toothpastes contain bases. These neutralise the acid.

The stings from many animals and plants contain acids or bases.
You can treat them by neutralisation.
Wasp stings can be treated with vinegar.
Bee stings can be treated with sodium bicarbonate.

a What do these treatments tell you about:
   i)   the pH value of a wasp sting?
   ii) the pH value of a bee sting?
Explain your answers carefully.

Getting metals

Iron ore can be **reduced** to iron.
This is done in a blast furnace.

b What does reduce mean?

▶ Look at this diagram of a blast furnace:
You may remember it from *Spotlight Science 8*.

The labels are shown here.
● molten iron ● molten slag ● waste gases
● hot air ● iron ore, coke and limestone
Your teacher will give you a copy of the diagram.
Write the labels on your diagram in the right place.
Do not write in this book.

c Why is iron so useful?

d Write about one problem of using iron.

Reduction can be a useful reaction.

Making quicklime

Here's a chance for *you* to carry out a useful reaction.

Take 2 limestone chips which look similar.
Heat one chip strongly in a hot Bunsen flame.
Heat it for 10 minutes. Then let the chip cool.
Compare the heated and unheated chips:

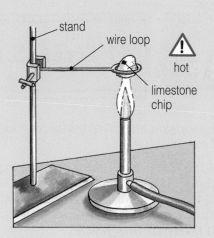

stand
wire loop
hot
limestone chip

* Appearance – what do they look like?
* Do they scratch easily? Use an iron nail to test.
  (Don't touch the solids.)
* Add 2 drops of water to each chip. Test the liquid with
  pH paper.
* Add one drop of dilute acid to each.

acid

Record all your results in a table.
Do you notice any difference between the chips?

When you heated the limestone chip it decomposed (broke down).
We call this reaction **thermal decomposition**.
Two products were made in the reaction:

| calcium carbonate $\longrightarrow$ calcium oxide + carbon dioxide |
| limestone   quicklime |

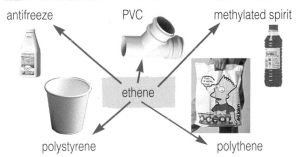

scratch test

add water

e What happened to the carbon dioxide?

f Quicklime is an alkali. Sometimes farmers use it on soil.
Why do you think this is?

Crude oil products

In Books 7 and 8 you learnt about crude oil. Crude oil is a mixture
of substances. These substances are separated in an oil refinery.
Ethene can be made from a substance in crude oil.
Look at some of ethene's useful reactions:

antifreeze   PVC   methylated spirit
ethene
polystyrene   polythene

▶ Look over pages 138 and 139. In your group decide which you
think is the most useful reaction. Say why.

---

1 Copy and complete using a word from
the box:

| neutralise   reduce   oxidise |
| copper   iron   bee   ethene   wasp |

a) Bases . . . . acids.
b) . . . . means take the oxygen from.
c) . . . . stings can be treated with acid.
d) . . . . is made in a blast furnace.
e) . . . . can be made into polythene.

2 We get iron from iron ore using a blast
furnace.
a) Use books to find out how some other
metals can be obtained from their ores.
b) Metals can be mixed together to make
alloys.
Why are alloys made?

3

The world would be a better place
without scientists. I'd like to turn the
clock back. We don't need all these
new chemicals. Why are scientists
still carrying out new reactions?
They're wasting our money.

Do you agree with Mr Grey?
If so, explain why.
If not, explain why not.

Things to do

What's the use?

In the last lesson you looked at useful reactions.
But are **all** reactions useful**?**

▶ Look at the clues. Each clue should help you find a new
word about burning.
Pick out the red letters to find a new word. What is it**?**
Ask your teacher for a blank puzzle sheet.
Do not write in this book.

- An element found in fuels. It has the symbol C. ——————▶
- A reaction in which heat (energy) is given out. ——————▶
- This is made up mostly of nitrogen and oxygen. ——————▶
- An element found in fuels and in water. ——————▶
- With fuel and oxygen it makes up the fire triangle. ——————▶
- These burn in oxygen to give us energy. ——————▶

A fuel burning is a useful reaction.

Burning fuels are spoiling our planet. You can't call that a useful reaction.

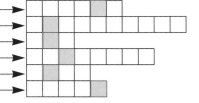

a Why does Emma think that burning is a useful reaction**?**

b Does this reaction spoil our planet**?** What does Jop mean**?**
(A look back at pages 4 and 5 may help you.)

▶ Look at these photos. They all show the results of a chemical
reaction. Say whether you think the reaction is **useful** or
not useful. Explain why.

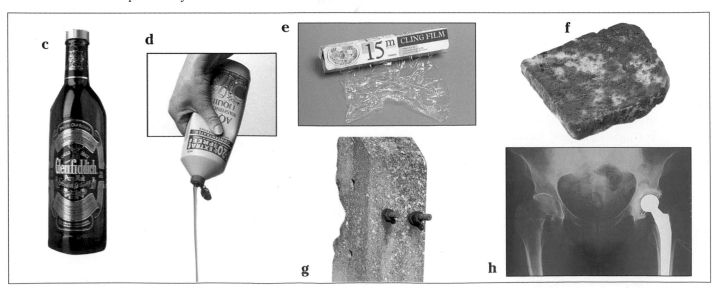

Going off

You wouldn't fancy eating the bread on page 140!
At home we need to store food and keep it fresh.
Microbes which cause decay need to be stopped from growing.
Slowing down the growth of microbes slows down the chemical
changes in food. But how can we do this? How can we **preserve**
our food?

In your group, make a list of ways to preserve food. The photos
may give you some clues. Say how you think each method works.
For example,

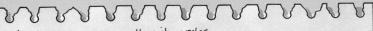

Way to preserve	How it works
Freezing	Slows down the rate at which microbes grow. Freezes the water the microbes need.

Use your group's ideas to plan an investigation.

Which method is best to preserve food?

Show your plan to your teacher.

Food additives

Chemical preservatives are used in some foods. These are
chemicals which poison microbes but are safe for humans.
Chemical preservatives are just one type of food additive.

i What other substances are added to foods?

j What is an E number?

k Why are people worried about food additives?

l Do *you* think additives are a good thing? Explain your views.

Things to do

1 Copy out each description of a reaction.
Which reaction best fits the description?
Match the reaction to its description.

Description	**Reaction**
• A useful reaction which can make some nasty products.	• Fermenting sugar
• A slow reaction which is not useful.	• Burning a fuel
• A slow reaction which makes alcohol.	• Rusting of iron

2 Plan an investigation to see what things
can change the rate at which a half-eaten
apple goes brown.

3 **GOVERNMENT BANS ALL
FLAVOURING ADDITIVES**

Look at foods in your home.
How would this ban affect the kind of foods
you eat?
Would you support this ban?

4

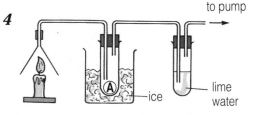

This apparatus collects the products as a
candle burns.
a) What collects in A?
b) What happens to the lime water? Why?
c) Write a word equation for the reaction.

Finding the energy

Do you enjoy November 5th?
Bonfire night is about chemical reactions!
▶ The chemical reactions in fireworks transfer energy.
    Write about all the energy transfers in the photo.

Most chemical reactions **give out** energy. They are called
exothermic reactions.
But some reactions **take in** energy from the surroundings.
These are called **endothermic** reactions.

Your mouth feels cold when you eat sherbet.
The reaction of sherbet with water is **endothermic**.
The reaction takes in heat energy from your mouth so it cools it
down.

Energy in or out?

Try some of these reactions. See what happens to the temperature.

1   Dissolve some citric acid in 50 cm³ water.
    Note the temperature of the solution.

    Add crushed limestone to the solution, one spatula measure
    at a time. Stir and note the temperature after each addition.
    Add 5 spatula measures in total.

    What do you notice?
    Is this an exothermic or endothermic reaction?

thermometer
crushed
limestone
citric acid
solution
⚠ eye protection

2   Repeat experiment 1 but add **sodium bicarbonate** instead
    of crushed limestone.

    What do you notice?
    Is this an exothermic or endothermic reaction?

sodium
bicarbonate
citric acid
solution
⚠ eye protection

3   Measure 25 cm³ of dilute sulphuric acid into a beaker.
    Note the temperature of the solution.

    Add 5 cm³ of sodium hydroxide solution to the acid. Stir and
    note the temperature of the solution. Repeat this until 30 cm³
    of sodium hydroxide have been added.

    What do you notice?
    Is this an exothermic or endothermic reaction?

measuring
cylinder
⚠ eye protection
sodium
hydroxide
solution
dilute
sulphuric
acid

4   Light a Bunsen burner.
    Natural gas burns.

    What do you notice?
    Is this an exothermic or endothermic reaction?

Do **not** measure
the temperature of
the flame. Just observe.

Lab in chaos

⚠️ eye protection

Five glass bottles are in the lab.
They all contain colourless liquids.
Four have lost their labels. One is labelled **dilute sulphuric acid**.

You have only 2 beakers and one thermometer.
How can you find out which of the 4 solutions are alkalis?
Write a plan for your teacher.
Have your plan checked. Then do it!

Energy is always transferred when a chemical change takes place.
Sometimes we can observe this
 – the temperature may change
 – we may see light or hear sound.

Think about these energy changes from chemical reactions.

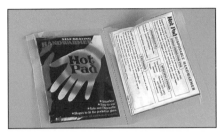

You may have seen these in camping shops.
They keep your hands warm for several hours.

a How do you think they work?

Have you ever bought one of these?
They are popular at outdoor concerts.

b How do you think they work?

c Why is this so useful?

But sometimes the energy transfer can be a problem.
Look at the newspaper extract.

d What should you do if you smell a gas leak?

Explosion wrecks home!

Workmen who picked their way through the rubble of a house demolished by a gas explosion yesterday found 94-year-old Mrs Ivy Shepherd still standing in the kitchen where she had been eating a cheese sandwich.
The roof and timbers had collapsed around Mrs Shepherd, a widow, but she was unharmed and her only complaint was of the dust in her white hair and a torn apron.
She was taken to hospital in Worthing, West Sussex, for a check-up but was later released.

---

1 Copy and complete:
a) Chemical reactions which give out energy are called . . . .
b) Chemical reactions which take in energy are called . . . .
c) In an . . . . reaction the temperature of the reaction mixture rises.
d) In an . . . . reaction the temperature of the reaction mixture falls.
e) Burning a fuel in air is an . . . . reaction.
f) Neutralisation is an . . . . reaction.
g) Dissolving sherbet in water is an . . . . reaction.

2 Spirit burners can be used to burn liquid fuels safely in the lab.
Plan an investigation to compare the amount of energy transferred when different fuels are burnt.

— burning fuel
— wick
— fuel

3 Is respiration an exothermic or endothermic reaction?
How do you know?

Things to do

What's your reaction?

In Books 7, 8 and 9 you have met lots of chemical reactions.

▶ Remind yourself of some reactions – copy and complete these word equations:

iron + oxygen ⟶ . . . . (rust)

. . . . + oxygen ⟶ magnesium oxide

iron oxide + carbon ⟶ . . . . + ...

acid + base ⟶ . . . . + water

fuel + oxygen ⟶ . . . . + ... + energy

a Which of the reactions above is:
i) combustion?
ii) neutralisation?

Nearly all the materials we use are made by chemical reactions.
Sometimes **elements** are made into **compounds**.

calcium + oxygen ⟶ calcium oxide

Sometimes **compounds** are made into new **compounds**.

copper carbonate ⟶ copper oxide + carbon dioxide

b What is an element?

c What is a compound?

d Which compound has the formula CaO?

e Which compound has the formula CO_2?

The future

But what about the future? New chemical reactions will make new materials.

. . . making petrol from paper?

It is possible to make oil from waste paper. At the moment the oil is just suitable for boiler fuel. But in the future it may be possible to change this to petrol and plastic.

. . . hydrogen to fuel a car?

The hydrogen reacts with oxygen to drive the engine.

. . . a cure for flu?

Scientists are using computers to help them design a molecule which may cure flu.

A best seller

- Make a class-book about **chemical reactions**.

- Your teacher will ask your group to write one section of the book.

- Design your pages carefully. They will need diagrams, cartoons and photos to make them interesting.

- Remember that someone will need to make the cover.

- What will your book be called?

Sections

oxidation

energy changes

physical change

combustion

reduction

respiration

rusting   fermentation

neutralisation

photosynthesis

word equations

chemical change

---

1 Copy and complete using a word from the box:

> reduce   oxygen   combustion
> neutralisation   fermentation

a) . . . . is a reaction in which a fuel burns in air.
b) . . . . means 'take away the oxygen from'.
c) . . . . is the making of alcohol from sugar.
d) Respiration uses . . . . gas.
e) . . . . is the reaction between an acid and a base.

2 Chemical reactions don't always happen. Think about the Reactivity Series. Predict whether a reaction will take place in each case.
a) magnesium + iron oxide
b) zinc oxide + copper
c) copper sulphate + zinc
d) magnesium sulphate + copper

3 Link the raw material in the list with the made material on the right, e.g. sand is used to make glass.

Raw material	Made material
sand	steel
oil	glass
iron ore	copper
malachite	paper
wood	plastic

4 Use books to find out how some of these things are made.
a) soap
b) bread
c) polythene
d) glass
e) yoghurt.

Things to do

Questions

1 Which of these are physical changes?
a) Adding water to orange squash.
b) Burning petrol in a car engine.
c) Making iron from iron ore.
d) Getting salt from sea water.
e) Making detergent from crude oil.

2 Gavin heated some magnesium ribbon in air.
He measured the mass of solid before and after heating.
Here are his results:

Mass of solid before heating = 0.24 g
Mass of solid after heating = 0.40 g

a) Copy and complete the word equation for the reaction:

magnesium + ... $\longrightarrow$ magnesium oxide

b) Name the solid product of the reaction.

c) Try to explain Gavin's results.

3 Explain how you could make a sample of solid magnesium sulphate starting with magnesium ribbon and dilute sulphuric acid.
Write a method. Draw diagrams.

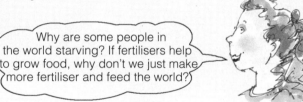

Why are some people in the world starving? If fertilisers help to grow food, why don't we just make more fertiliser and feed the world?

4 Can you help Sara to understand the problems?
Write down your thoughts.

5 Name the salts you make in these reactions:
a) iron + sulphuric acid
b) zinc carbonate + sulphuric acid
c) magnesium oxide + nitric acid
d) sodium hydroxide + hydrochloric acid

6 Stomach powders help to neutralise acids in your stomach.
Plan an investigation to find out which stomach powder is the best value for money.

7 Handwarmers are okay, but . . . .
Invent some self-warming soup for winter walks.
a) Design a can of soup which can warm itself when opened.
b) Make an advertisement for your invention.

8 Can scientists help to solve some of the world's problems?
Imagine **you** could make some new materials to solve these problems.
What would you want your new materials to do?
Make a list of your ideas.

Electricity and Magnetism

Electricity is important to all of us.
Our lives would be very different without it.

We use electricity to transfer energy from one place to another.
We use it for lighting and for heating.

And we can use electricity to make magnets – which we use
every day in radios, TVs, and many other things.

Electric charges

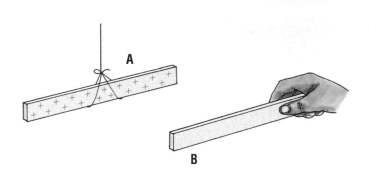

▶ Look at the diagram. It shows an acetate ruler **A**, hanging from a string:

It has been rubbed with a dry cloth, so it is **charged** with static electricity.
The acetate is **positively** charged (**+**).

Another acetate ruler **B** is rubbed with a dry cloth.

a What kind of charge will it have**?**

b What happens if it is held near one end of ruler **A?**

Then a strip of polythene is rubbed with a dry cloth.
Polythene gets the opposite kind of charge.

c What kind of charge does the polythene have**?**

d What happens if the polythene is held near one end of ruler **A?**

e What would happen if a charged polythene strip is brought near another charged polythene strip**?**

f Copy the table, and complete it using these 2 words:
repel   attract

g Why is it important to use a **dry** cloth**?**

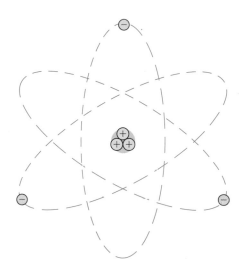

		First strip	
		acetate	polythene
Second strip	acetate		
	polythene		

The electron theory

All materials are made up of very small particles, called **atoms** (see also page 29).
Atoms contain both positive and negative charges.
The diagram shows what we think an atom is like:

The centre of an atom is called the **nucleus**. It has tiny particles called **protons**. These are **positive** ⊕.

h How many protons are there in the diagram**?**

Round the outside of the atom are the **electrons**. These are **negative** ⊖. They are spread in orbits round the nucleus.

i How many electrons are there in the diagram**?**

If the number of electrons ⊖ is equal to the number of protons ⊕, then the atom is **un**charged or **neutral**.

The electrons do not always stay with the atom. They can be removed. This is what happens when you rub the plastic with the cloth.

Using the electron theory

Let's see what happens when you charge a plastic ruler by rubbing it.

Before you rub the ruler it is uncharged and neutral.
This is because all the atoms are neutral.
Each atom has the same number of protons $\oplus$ and electrons $\ominus$. The $\oplus$ and $\ominus$ charges are balanced.

j Count the number of $\oplus$ and $\ominus$ charges on each of these 2 neutral objects:
What do you find?

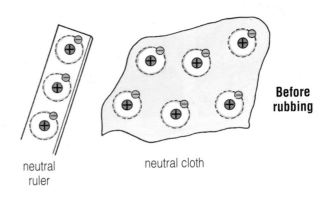

Before rubbing

neutral ruler   neutral cloth

After you rub the ruler, it is charged (positive).
The charges are **un**balanced.
Some electrons have moved **from** the ruler **to** the cloth.
The cloth has gained extra electrons, so it is negative.
The ruler has lost electrons, so it is positive.

k Count the number of charges on each object now:
What do you find?

Notice that:
- The rubbing has not made any extra charges. It has just separated them.
- It is only the negative charges (electrons) that move. The positive charges are fixed inside the atoms.

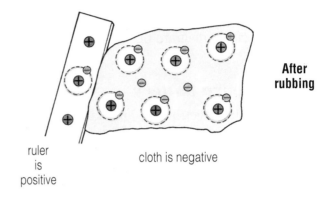

After rubbing

ruler is positive   cloth is negative

▶ Now draw similar diagrams to show what happens when you rub a polythene strip and it becomes negative.

Electricity on the move

You have seen a Van de Graaff generator used to charge up objects and people.

Your teacher will show you what happens when an ammeter is connected,
- to a battery
- to the Van de Graaff generator, as shown:

What happens? What conclusion can you make?

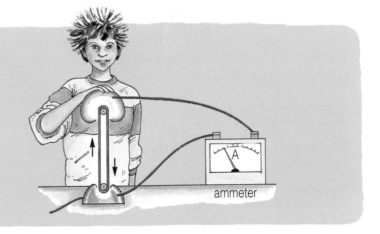

ammeter

---

1 Copy and complete:
a) If charges are the same sign (+ or −), then they . . . . each other.
b) If charges are different signs, then they . . . . each other.
c) The centre of an atom is called the . . . . It contains positive charges called . . . .
d) In orbit round the nucleus are the . . . . charges, called . . . .
e) In a neutral atom, the number of . . . . equals the number of . . . .
f) Only . . . . charges can move.

2 When Joanne brushes her long dry hair, it fluffs out. Explain why this happens.

3 Explain why you think electrons are pushed out of the negative (−) terminal of a battery and not the positive (+) terminal.

4 A scientist makes a new plastic called 'Plazzy'. Design experiments to find out:
a) whether Plazzy becomes positively or negatively charged when rubbed with cloth,
b) whether Plazzy is an electrical conductor.

Things to do

In series

▶ The diagram shows a circuit with 2 bulbs in **series**:

a What does each symbol stand for?

b What can you say about the current through **A** and the current through **B?**

c What happens if bulb **B** breaks? Why?

d Draw a circuit diagram of 3 bulbs in series.

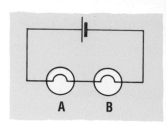

Bulbs in series

Energy from a battery

A battery pushes electrons (−) round the circuit:

e The electrons come out of the negative (−) terminal and not the positive terminal. Why do you think this is?

The flow of electrons is called a **current**. The size of the current is measured in amperes (amps, A).

f What meter would you use to measure the current?

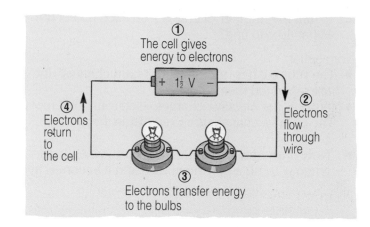

① The cell gives energy to electrons

② Electrons flow through wire

④ Electrons return to the cell

③ Electrons transfer energy to the bulbs

The electrons carry energy with them. The higher the **voltage** of the battery, the more energy the electrons have:

g What meter would you use to measure the voltage?

The energy of the electrons is used to heat up the filament in the bulb, so it gives out light.

h Draw an Energy Transfer Diagram for this circuit.

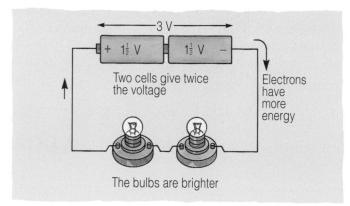

3 V

+ 1½ V   1½ V −

Two cells give twice the voltage

Electrons have more energy

The bulbs are brighter

A conductor lets electrons pass through it easily. It has a low **resistance**.
An insulator has a high resistance. The electrons cannot move through the insulator, so there is no current.

i Write down the names of 3 conductors and 3 insulators.

▶ Here are some of the symbols used in circuit diagrams.

j Copy the symbols and label each one.

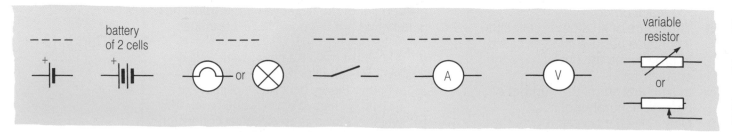

battery of 2 cells

or

A

V

variable resistor

or

Reading ammeters

The diagrams show two ammeters:

What are the readings **k, l, m, n, o,** and **p?**

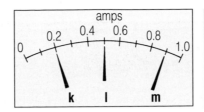

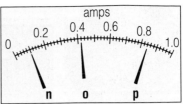

Measuring currents

Here is a series circuit:

- Draw a circuit diagram for it.

- Then connect up the circuit. Make sure the + terminal of the ammeter is connected to the + terminal of the battery.

- Adjust the variable resistor to make the bulb as bright as possible.
  What is the reading on the ammeter?

- Disconnect the ammeter and then re-connect it in position 2.
  What is the reading now?
  What is the reading on the ammeter if it is in position 3?
  Write a sentence to describe what you found.

- Now connect a second bulb in **series**.
  What happens to the brightness of the first bulb?
  What happens to the current through the ammeter?
  Explain why you think this happens, using the words:
  current   electrons   resistance

- Predict what would happen if you added a third bulb in series. Try it if you can.

- With just one bulb, use the variable resistor to reduce the current until the bulb is not quite glowing.
  What is the reading on your ammeter now?

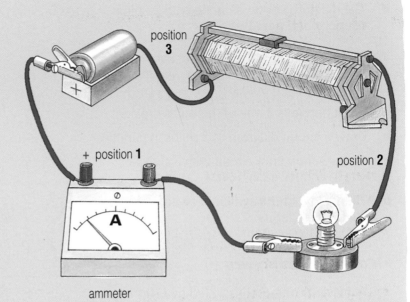

ammeter

A digital ammeter

Position of ammeter	Current (amps)
1	
2	
3	

---

1 Copy and complete:
In a **series** circuit,
a) The current is the . . . . through each part of the circuit.
b) If you add extra bulbs, the current is . . . . and the bulbs are . . . . bright.
c) If you add extra cells, the electrons have . . . . energy and bulbs shine . . . . brightly.
d) An ammeter measures the . . . . in a circuit, in . . . . or A.
e) A battery pushes . . . . round a circuit. The size of the push is measured in . . . . , by using a . . . .
f) A good conductor has a . . . . resistance.

2 An ammeter is connected in series with a battery, a switch and a bulb.
a) Draw the circuit diagram.
b) If the ammeter reads 0.8 A, how much current passes through the bulb?
c) A second bulb is connected in series. Draw the circuit diagram.
d) The ammeter reading is now 0.4 A. How much current passes through each bulb now?
e) Explain why this current is less than before.

3 The ampere and the volt are named after André Ampère and Alessandro Volta. Find out more about these people and what they did.

Things to do

In parallel

▶ The diagram shows a circuit with 2 bulbs connected in **parallel**:

When the electrons travel from the battery, *some* of them go through bulb **A**, and the rest of them go through bulb **B**.

a What happens if one of the bulbs breaks**?**

b Draw a circuit diagram of 3 bulbs in parallel.

c Now re-draw your circuit with 3 switches, one to control each bulb.

d Then add a fourth switch to switch off all the bulbs together.

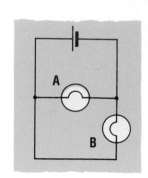

Bulbs in parallel

Measuring currents

• Connect up this circuit, with the **ammeter** in position 1:
Take care to connect the ammeter correctly.

• What is the reading on your ammeter**?**

• Then connect the ammeter in position 2. What is the current through bulb **A?**

• Then find the current in position 3.

• What do you notice about your results? Explain this, using these words:
current   electrons   resistance

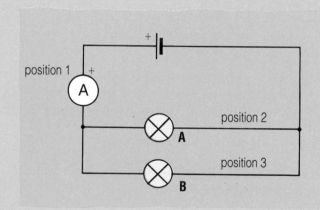

Measuring voltages

Here is a cell connected to a bulb.
A **voltmeter** is connected *in parallel* with the bulb:

A voltmeter is always connected in parallel with part of a circuit. It measures the voltage across that part of the circuit.

• Connect 2 bulbs in **parallel** with a battery. Then use a voltmeter to measure the voltage across each part of the circuit. What do you find**?**

• Then connect 2 bulbs in **series** with a battery, and measure the voltage across each part. What do you find now**?**

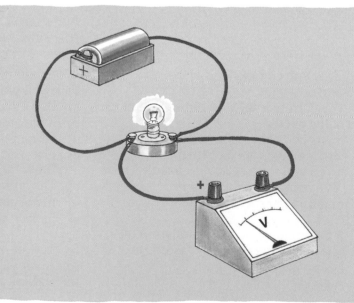

Analysing circuits

Here is a circuit diagram for 2 lights in a doll's house:

Use your finger to follow the path of the electrons from the battery through the bulb **A** and back to the battery. *If your finger has to go through a switch, then this switch is needed to put on the light*.

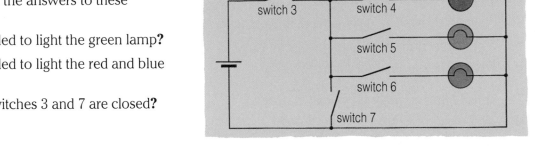

e Which switch is needed to turn on bulb **A**?

f Which switch is needed for bulb **B**?

Use the same method to find the answers to these questions:

g Which switches are needed to light the green lamp**?**

h Which switches are needed to light the red and blue lamps together**?**

i What happens if both switches 3 and 7 are closed**?**

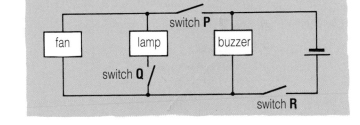

j How can you switch on the buzzer and the lamp**?**

k What happens if only switches **P** and **R** are closed**?**

l Re-draw the circuit so that the fan, lamp and buzzer each have their own switch.

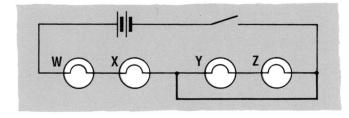

In this circuit, 2 of the lamps have been **short-circuited** by a thick wire:

m What happens when the switch is closed**?**

n Re-draw the circuit so only lamp **Z** is short-circuited.

Things to do

1 Copy and complete:
a) In a . . . . circuit there is more than one path for the electrons to flow.
b) A voltmeter is always connected in . . . . with part of a circuit.

2 Here is a circuit with 3 ammeters:

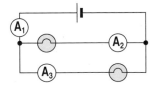

If ammeter A$_1$ shows 0.5 A and A$_2$ shows 0.3 A, what is the reading on A$_3$?

3 Draw a circuit diagram to show how two 6 volt bulbs can be lit brightly from two 3 volt cells.

4 Draw a circuit containing a battery, switch and 3 bulbs labelled, A, B and C. Bulbs A and B are in series, and C is in parallel with A. The switch controls only bulb C. When all the bulbs are lit, which one is the brightest?

5 In these circuits, all the bulbs are the same:

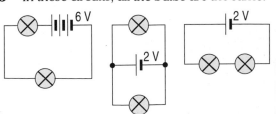

a) Which circuit has the dimmest bulbs?
b) Explain why this is, using the words:
current   voltage   resistance

153

Magnetic fields

You can use a magnet to pick up paper-clips, but not paper.
Paper is not magnetic.

a Which of these are magnetic: wood, iron, plastic, steel,
cloth, a coin, copper wire**?**

The diagram shows a magnet on a cork, floating on water:

b Which direction will the magnet point to**?**

c What is the name of this instrument**?**

The ends of the bar magnet are called **poles**.

d Which end of a magnet is the N-pole**?**

e If another magnet is brought near, so that its N-pole is
near the N-pole of this magnet, what happens**?**

f What happens if a S-pole is brought near a N-pole**?**

We say that: **Like poles repel,
Unlike poles attract**.

a magnet on a floating cork

The magnets exert a force on each other without touching.
This is because a magnet has a **magnetic field** round it.
Iron and steel are affected by a magnetic field.

The Earth has a magnetic field round it. This field makes
a compass point to the North.

We cannot see a magnetic field, but we can plot a map of it.

Plotting magnetic fields

Put a magnet under a sheet of paper, as shown:

Sprinkle a few iron filings over the paper, and then
tap the paper. The iron filings act like tiny compasses.

Look carefully at the pattern that appears:

- Sketch the shape of this field.
  The curved lines are called **field lines** or lines of force.

- Use a small 'plotting compass' to follow a field line
  from the N-pole to the S-pole.

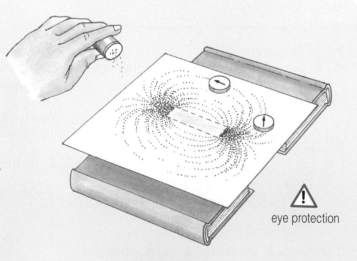

eye protection

Now find the shape of the magnetic field when
2 magnets are placed in line, with
a) The two N-poles near each other like this:
b) A N-pole near a S-pole.
Your teacher can give you a Help Sheet.

Electro-magnetism

In 1820, a Danish scientist called Hans Oersted discovered that:
an electric current produces a magnetic field.

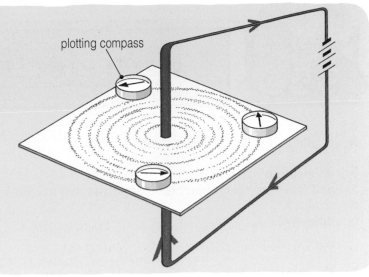
plotting compass

In this experiment, a large current is passed up the thick copper wire.
Iron filings are sprinkled on the card to show the shape of the magnetic field:

Plotting compasses show the direction of the field lines.

g   What happens if the current is reversed?

h   What happens to the compasses when the current is switched off?

The magnetic field from a single wire is very weak. To make it stronger, the wire is made into a **coil**, or **solenoid**.

The field round a coil

Iron filings are sprinkled on a card round a coil:

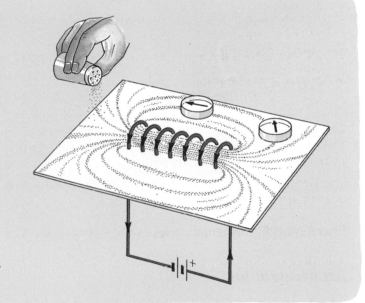

i   What happens when the current is switched on?

j   What do you notice about the shape of the magnetic field?   (Hint: see the opposite page.)

The compasses show the direction of the magnetic field.

k   What happens if the current is reversed?

l   What happens to the compasses when the current is switched off?

A coil like this is an **electro-magnet**.
An electromagnet usually has an iron **core**, which becomes magnetised and makes a stronger electromagnet.

You will use an electromagnet in the next lesson.

---

1   Copy and complete:
a)   Like poles . . . .   Unlike poles . . . .
b)   The Earth has a magnetic . . . . round it.
c)   A magnetic . . . . can be produced by an electric . . . .
d)   The . . . . field round a straight . . . . is in the shape of circles.
e)   The field round a coil (or . . . .) has the same shape as the . . . . round a bar . . . .
f)   An electromagnet only works if a . . . . is flowing through the . . . .

2   Drink cans are usually made from either steel or aluminium. In a metal re-cycling plant they need to be separated. Design a machine to do this.

3   In the diagrams below, **A, B, C, D** are compasses. In diagram (a), a current is flowing **down**, into the paper.
In diagram (b), there is no current flowing.
Copy the diagrams and draw in the direction of each compass needle.

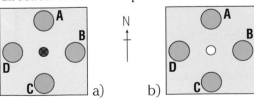

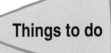
Things to do

4   Plan an investigation to see if iron can be made into a magnet more easily than steel. How would you make it a fair test?

Using electromagnets

▶ Explain what is happening in this photo:

Is it an electromagnet or a permanent magnet?
In what ways are electromagnets and permanent magnets
a similar?
b different?

Investigating electromagnets

Plan an investigation to find out *what affects the strength of an electromagnet*.

- What things can you vary?
  Choose *one* of these, and plan your investigation.

- How will you make it a fair test?

- How will you measure the strength of your electromagnet?

Show your plan to your teacher, and then do it.
!Do not use electricity at more than 12 volts!

- If you have time, investigate the other variables.

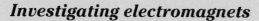

Electromagnets have many uses.

An electric bell

This is used in doorbells, burglar alarms, and fire-bells.

Study the diagram:

c When the switch is closed, there is a complete circuit. What happens to the electromagnet?

The iron bar is on a springy metal strip which can bend.

d What happens to the iron bar?
e What happens to the hammer?

There is now a gap in the circuit, because the iron bar is not touching the contact.

f What happens now?

g Why does the bell ring for as long as the switch is closed?

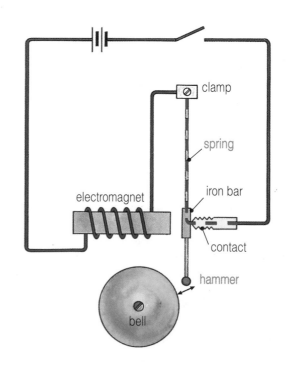

clamp

spring

electromagnet

iron bar

contact

hammer

bell

A relay

This is a switch operated by an electromagnet.
It is used when you want to use a small current
to switch on a larger current.

Study the diagram:

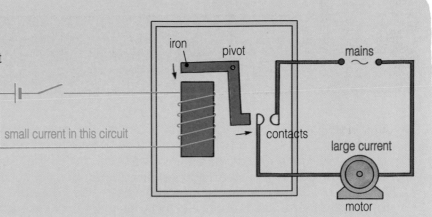

small current in this circuit

There are 2 circuits here.

h When a current flows in the blue circuit,
what happens to the core of the coil?

i What happens to the iron bar?

j What happens to the contacts in the
red circuit?

k What happens to the motor?

The motor might be the starter-motor in a car, or
the motor in a washing-machine, or in an electric train.

A circuit-breaker

This is an automatic safety switch.
It cuts off the current if it gets too big.

Study the diagram:

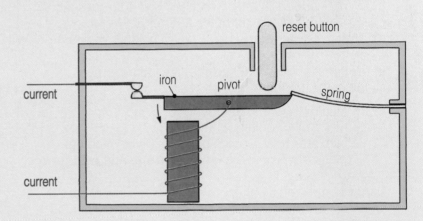

l What happens to the electromagnet when
the current is flowing?

m If the current is big, what happens to
the iron bar?

n What does this do to the current?

o How would you re-set this circuit-breaker?

p To make it switch off at a lower current,
how would you change the electromagnet?

Electromagnets are also used in loudspeakers, in motors, in cassette-recorders,
and in computers to store data on the computer discs.

---

1 Copy and complete:
The strength of an electromagnet can be
increased by:
a) increasing the number of turns on the . . . . ,
b) increasing the . . . . , or
c) using an . . . . core.

2 Design a relay that would use a small
current to turn **off** a big current. Draw a
labelled diagram of your design.

3 Door-chimes use an electromagnet to
make a 'bing-bong' sound. When the switch
is pushed, an iron rod hits one chime (a metal
tube). When the switch is released, the rod
springs back to hit the other chime tube.
Draw a labelled diagram to show how this
could work.

4 Design a machine that could separate full
and empty milk-bottles on a conveyor belt.

Things to do

Questions

Ben Franklin

1 Benjamin Franklin (1706–1790) was a scientist who helped to write the American Declaration of Independence ("... *we hold these truths to be self-evident: that all men are created equal*..."). He risked his life flying a kite in a storm and invented the lightning conductor.
  a) Find out all you can about him, and what he discovered.
  b) How have our ideas about electricity changed since he was alive?

2 This circuit is used to dim a light:

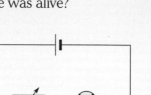

While the light is being dimmed, what happens to
  a) The current in the lamp?
  b) The resistance of the variable resistor?
  c) The voltage across the lamp?

3 The diagram shows an electrical circuit:

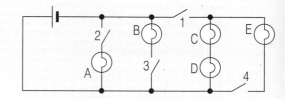

  a) What happens if only switch 1 is closed?
  b) What happens if only switches 3 and 4 are closed?
  c) How would you light bulbs A, C and D?
  d) If all the switches are closed, which bulb(s) are dimmest? Why?

4 In the circuits shown, all the cells are identical, and all the bulbs are identical:

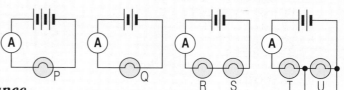

  a) Which bulb would be brightest? Why?
  b) Which bulb would not be lit? Why?
  c) Which ammeter would show the lowest reading? Explain why, using the words **voltage** and **resistance**.

5 Danny connected a battery in series with a switch, an ammeter, a variable resistor and a coil of wire. Then he connected a voltmeter to measure the voltage across the coil.

  a) Draw a circuit diagram of his circuit.

The table shows his results as he altered the variable resistor:

  b) Plot a large graph of the current against the voltage, drawing the line of 'best fit'.
  c) Which result(s) do you think could be wrong and should be checked?
  d) What would be the current if the voltage was 8.4 V?
  e) What conclusion(s) can you draw from the graph?

Current (A)	0.4	0.7	1.2	1.5	1.9	2.4	2.8
Voltage (V)	1.9	2.9	4.9	6.3	8.0	10.1	11.8

6 Rachel tested 2 electromagnets, one with 20 turns and one with 60 turns on the coil. She counted how many nails each electromagnet could hold up at different currents. Here are her results:

Current (A)		0	0.5	1.0	1.5	2.0	2.5	3.0	3.5	4.0
Number of nails	20-turns	0	1	4	9	15	21	27	33	38
	60-turns	0	4	12	27	42	55	61	64	64

  a) Plot a graph for each electromagnet (on the same axes).
  b) Describe what happens when the current is increased in
    i) the 20-turn coil,
    ii) the 60-turn coil.
  c) Can you explain this?

Index